AMERICAN EXPLORATION AND TRAVEL

On the Oregon Trail

Robert Stuart's Journey of Discovery

On the

OREGON TRAIL

*Robert Stuart's
Journey of Discovery*

Edited by Kenneth A. Spaulding

UNIVERSITY OF OKLAHOMA PRESS : NORMAN

Library of Congress Catalog Card Number : 53-8814

Copyright 1953 by the University of Oklahoma Press, Publishing Division of the University. Composed and Printed at Norman, Oklahoma, U.S.A., by the University of Oklahoma Press. First edition.

for
Bess and Steve

Preface

One of the greatest rewards received by one who edits a book like this is the rediscovery of the people who make it possible. Librarians, teachers, and others without any professional relationship to the fields of scholarship lend time and encouragement far beyond the limits of obligation, knowing as they do so that they will have no reward except the real though disinterested pleasure of adding to human understanding. Because this work would have been quite impossible without such assistance, I wish to express my deep sense of gratitude for their contributions.

First of all, I wish to express my indebtedness to the Library Committee of the Yale University Library and to James E. Babb, librarian, for granting me permission to work with the Stuart manuscript. I wish also to thank the staff of the Yale University Library and particularly Dorothy W. Bridgwater, assistant reference librarian, for aid that was more than merely competent.

Albertine Loomis of Detroit has generously allowed me to use the letter by Elisha Loomis describing an address given by Robert Stuart. Lewis Beeson, secretary of the Michigan Historical Commission, Margaret I. Smith, chief reference librarian of the General Library at the University of Michigan, and Barbara Kell, reference librarian for the Missouri Historical Society, all contributed illustrative material of value. Jay B. Hubbell, in his capacity as editor of *American Literature,* made available for use material from that publication.

There were others who contributed astute suggestions, or took the trouble to provide needed information. Esther Loughin of the Michigan Local and Family History Section of the Michigan State Library, Elleine H. Stones, chief of the Burton Historical Collection of the Detroit Public Library, F. Clever Bald, assistant director of the Michigan Historical Collections at the University of Michigan, and Floyd C. Shoemaker, secretary of the State Historical Society of Missouri, all made generous and valuable comments. Leonard F. Dean, head of the English Department at the University of Connecticut, shared his own experience freely as well as striving to create the conditions under which such work as this becomes possible.

To Alexander Kern and Merrill Heiser, both of the English Department of the University of Iowa, I owe another kind of debt. They saw this venture through its formative stages, offering guidance, restraint, and above all, encouragement when it was most needed.

To my family I owe the greatest debt of all. I am grateful to my wife Elizabeth for belief which seemed never to fail; I am grateful to my son Stephen because during the most difficult moments he managed to tolerate his father.

Kenneth A. Spaulding

Union, Connecticut
June 21, 1953

Contents

Preface   *ix*

Editor's Introduction   3

On the Oregon Trail
  Robert Stuart's Journey of Discovery
  June 1812   27
  July 1812   44
  August 1812   69
  September 1812   90
  October 1812   108
  November 1812   128
  December 1812   132
  January 1813   141
  March 1813   142
  April 1813   149

Appendix I
  The Manuscript of the
  "Travelling Memoranda"   165

Appendix II
  Letter by Elisha Loomis Relating an Account
  Given by Robert Stuart of His Journey   170

A Selected Bibliography   181

Index   185

Illustrations

Robert Stuart   *facing page*   18
Indian Canoe, The Dalles   34
Astoria in 1811   50
A Crow Lodge   82
Page from Stuart's Manuscript   98
The Mouth of the Platte   130
Sawyer s and Planters in the Missouri   146
Item from the *Missouri Gazette*   162

Map: The Route Followed by Stuart from Astoria
     to St. Louis   *on pages*   24–25

On the Oregon Trail

Robert Stuart's Journey of Discovery

Editor's Introduction

I

ROBERT STUART was an American by choice. Born in Callander, Scotland, in 1785, he had made his way to Canada by the time he was twenty-two. Here, perhaps with the aid of an uncle who had preceded him, he found employment as a clerk in the North West Company, the younger of the two British fur-trading concerns. In this way he was early settled on the continent and in the trade which was to hold his interest for most of his life.

But Canada was not to be the end of the journey for Stuart. Three years after his arrival in North America he was pushing south to join John Jacob Astor's Pacific Fur Company, a group pledged to the bold enterprise of combating the British companies out in the far regions of the Columbia River. It was by this act that Stuart allied himself to Astor, whose aims were patriotic as well as commercial, and to the United States. His allegiance to the country of his adoption was to remain steadfast for the remainder of his life.

To a man of Stuart's temperament and circumstances, the United States must have offered a very strong appeal in the early part of the nineteenth century. Seldom has there been a time so favorable to men who were strong in character as well as in the acquisitive instinct. To the people of a young

3

and rapidly expanding nation, a single venture often appeared to enclose both the interests of the nation and the interests of the entrepreneur. Business was the medium through which the nation would grow, and to be enterprising in commerce was therefore to be patriotic. Even Jefferson looked to private property as a means of insuring the perpetuation of individual liberty, believing that citizens who owned their small farms would never be slaves: those who themselves controlled the means of getting their livelihood could not, he thought, be the victims of coercion.

Then there was always the possibility that England, France, or Spain might intensify their efforts to expand their present holdings in North America. All three were firmly established on the North American continent, and a change of government in London, Paris, or Madrid might at any time bring with it an increased interest in American possessions. There was need for haste.

Consequently, the occupation of new land was a patriotic act, as well as a way to a better living. The welfare of nation and the individual were the same, it being self-evident that he who served one served the other. The sense of duty to country, the desire to win public approval, and the urge to make a better living all combined in a single compulsion that sent men westward toward another sea.

To a young man at the beginning of his life the new nation must have seemed rich in promise. Robert Stuart's father had been a Scottish crofter, a sometime teacher who died in his middle years after more than three decades of struggle. Robert himself had grown up in a country where land, even the poorest, had for the most part been pre-empted centuries before his birth. Since land was the primary means of gaining a living, the difficulty of acquiring even the most barren acres meant that life was a struggle for those who achieved no more than a state of moderate poverty. And

Robert, the third of nine children, could not have looked for much by way of an inheritance. For this reason coming to America was for him, as for so many other young Scotsmen, a move dictated by prudence as well as by love of adventure.

In contrast, he now found himself confronting a continent that promised very solid rewards to the enterprising. Here were millions of acres of free land, and fortunes to be made in commerce. There were difficulties, to be sure. Weather, geography, and human weakness conspired against the adventurer, and rascality existed here as elsewhere. But these were surmountable obstacles for the man who was strong in body and character, willing to enlist his whole being in the effort to serve himself and the future. For a young Scot there was another advantage that must have seemed important: in this endeavor, no moral compromises were necessary. The struggle was in essence between man and nature rather than between man and man; it was possible to subdue the wilderness without running afoul of the Biblical injunction as to how we shall treat our neighbor, and to be humanly just without endangering success. Where patriotism and self-interest urged a young man onward, morality offered no bar.

If this conception was in Stuart's mind during the first months after his arrival in Canada, later events were to justify it. The rigorous beliefs manifested by him on the harrowing journey from Astoria to St. Louis were actually a reason for the venture's success; it was his steady, impersonal application of principle that allowed him to control his party without arousing resentment, for apparently the other members knew that of the seven he was invariably the last to receive personal consideration. Stuart brought to his new life the beliefs acquired in the old, and found that they earned him not only inner assurance but the quality of leadership as well.

The immediate reasons for his move to New York are not known. But the North West Company required apprenticeships of seven years to be served by clerks before they were eligible for promotion to partnerships, with no assurance of advancement at the end of the term, while in the United States the prospects were brighter. John Jacob Astor was searching for experienced fur traders to carry out a new enterprise, the Pacific Fur Company. This group was to set up an establishment at the mouth of the Columbia River, with subsidiary posts at promising points along the headwaters. Here they were to enter into competition with the North West Company and the Hudson's Bay Company, attempting to break the British monopoly on trade in the Columbia drainage and, more than incidentally, to locate an American settlement on the Pacific Coast. In 1810 it was possible to conceive that the United States might one day extend that far, a belief strongly suggested by Astor in his letters to President Jefferson on the subject of his Columbian project.

Stuart was hired and soon became a partner in the new company, a fact that must have served as a convincing argument in favor of his recent change of employment. In this manner he began his association with his adopted country, which offered him, in addition to seemingly boundless natural resources, the advantage of a dynamic society in which there were possibilities for advancement of a kind to be found not even in Canada, where some of the social stratifications of Europe were still traceable in the organization of the fur companies. At the age of twenty-five, Stuart may have perceived that the son of a poor crofter who wished not only to make money but to stand well in a community of citizens would find his opportunity in the United States.

If these were the reasons for his decision, the future showed him to have been wise. The man who was once a young and very obscure clerk in the service of the North West Company lived to be a well-to-do and much respected citizen of Detroit, where he served as a judge and as an elder in the

Presbyterian church. In his achievement there was nothing with which he needed to reproach himself: the records indicate that he was both stern and just, that he was capable of anger, but not without cause. His middle years were spent in the wild regions of peninsular Michigan, where his duties consisted in part of keeping in check the unruly woodsmen who wished to argue their accounts, advise him concerning the conduct of the company, or merely celebrate their arrival at the post. In such rough company he was able to make himself respected as a man and at the same time to lay the groundwork for his later financial success. He continued his service in the American Fur Company until 1834, the year when Astor sold his holdings, and then moved to Detroit to engage in speculation in land. By the time of his death in 1848 he had become a participant in the financing of canal construction, another investment popular in early nineteenth-century America.

Throughout his career Stuart adhered to the enterprises closely related to the interests of the growing nation. From 1810, when he journeyed down the Hudson to New York and around Cape Horn to Astoria, until about 1840, American fur traders saw the period of their greatest prosperity. Prior to 1810 there had been no extensive trading west of the Mississippi, the area being almost unknown until Lewis and Clark returned in 1806; after the thirties the demand for pelts declined rapidly. But before it subsided, the demand for fur had led the trappers and traders to and across the Rockies, forerunners in the restless movements of discovery that characterized the first half of the century.

Stuart's business interests, though not so spectacular, were in their way as illustrative of national development. Land speculation followed close upon discovery; restless settlers, spurred by hopes, rumors, or frustrations, sold their acres to men who could afford to await the coming of farm communities and towns. The second group of owners planned either to put the land to actual use or to sell it to those who would. But before the land could be made productive, there had to be a means of bringing to it the necessary tools and of carrying the resulting products to market. Interest in transportation appeared soon after the possession of land had led to a desire to see it utilized, one of the results being the construction of a complex system of canals and waterways enabling farmers and manufacturers to ship their products from the Chicago area to New York. Like his investments in land, Stuart's commitments to inland transport showed his undeviating faculty for remaining close to the center of national economic interest. The relationship is, in fact, so close that his personal career could almost be read as a pattern of the nation's interests.

Seen in this way, Robert Stuart takes on a representative look. But before he begins to appear as the nineteenth-century version of economic man, it should be remembered that he was far more than a kind of business sport, the product of a fortunate coincidence of person, time, and place. A human being stood behind the financial success, and it was he who was ultimately responsible. In order to succeed he had to act, and the design for action came from within.

Stuart was a compound of hardy boyhood, thrifty upbringing, and rigorous moral conceptions. Other factors are perceptible, too. There is intelligence, and the will to range far in order to find what is satisfactory. This implies, of course, the refusal to accept what is less than satisfactory. A glint of humor appears here and there in his account of the terrible journey from Astoria to St. Louis: he once refers to his tired old horse as a Rosinante and may by extension have had a quick glimpse of himself as Quixote. In moments of crisis there is sometimes the flash of temper, but instead of deciding his actions, it serves to charge his carefully chosen words with vigor, being always under his control. And there is pride, though pride too is kept subordinate to the perception of what is prudent and reasonable in any situation. Reason, strength of will, a high moral sense: these are the virtues that appear and reappear in Stuart's carefully stated sentences.

Robert Stuart was an American because he had a deep affinity for this countryside and this nation. He sought the United States because it was here that he found what he needed—the opportunity to rise financially and socially without trespassing upon his own moral conceptions or the rights of others. Although he took full advantage of his opportunities, he did not forget to give a full measure of loyal service in return, devoting himself to the causes of religion and education as well as to the cause of filling his own pockets. A plain man and a hard one when justice required him to be, he nevertheless escaped the inner hardness which robs its possessor of humanity. His fellows sometimes irritated and occasionally amused him, but he never made the mistake of holding them cheaply. In this affirmative conception he was at one with such Americans as Jefferson and Jackson—at one, and properly at home in their country.

I I

ROBERT STUART left Fort Astoria on June 29, 1812, with dispatches to be delivered to Astor in New York City. During the two years that had elapsed since the departure of the first party for Oregon no word of the venture had been carried back, the officials in the East being left without knowledge either of the contingent carried around the Horn in Astor's ship, the *Tonquin,* or of the group marching westward under the leadership of Wilson P. Hunt. It was therefore vital that they should be informed first of the fate of the men and second of what was required at the fort. Since all supplies and reinforcements came by ship from New York, the party at Astoria could be adequately equipped for the contingencies encountered after their arrival only by putting a list of requirements in Astor's hands. This was the mission that Stuart now proposed to accomplish.

The obstacles that were to confront him are almost beyond exaggeration. He had, first of all, the whole body of the Rocky Mountains to find a way through. These great upthrusts of foothills, shale, rock, and snow rose in jagged walls before him for every one of the more than seven hundred miles between eastern Oregon and eastern Wyoming, ascending at one part of the journey to altitudes of nearly eleven thousand feet. In the process of accomplishing their passage, he and his party were to combat extreme heat and cold, starvation, thirst, deep snow, warring Indians, madness, and even the threat of cannibalism. Yet they persisted. If the difficulties were so great on one occasion that Stuart no longer seems to have cared whether he lived or died, the mission remained, a matter of duty not only to Astor but to the men they had left behind.

The situation as Stuart knew it to be at Fort Astoria was precarious enough to provide a powerful stimulus. It was, in fact, even worse than he knew, for a few days before his departure Congress had declared war on Great Britain, an act that was later to enable the North West Company to enlist the aid of British warships in capturing the post. But he did know that, when the Astorians had arrived two years previously at the site on which they were to build, a party from the rival company was encamped only thirty miles up the Columbia, the race for the strategic location at the mouth of the river having been won and lost by that margin. Having failed in the first move, the British seemed more determined than ever to be rid of competition. From that moment, a steady pressure was exerted by them, for they understood, as did the Americans, that rights would be determined by possession. The only legal basis for commercial activities in the wilderness was a treaty negotiated in 1794 allowing nationals of both countries to trade with Indians living in territories controlled by either. But since Oregon was not to be specifically the subject of an agreement until 1818, the vague affirmations of the earlier document were easily ignored. Since the interested companies were themselves the only agencies for enforcement, Oregon in fact belonged to nobody. Being first and more strongly in the field, the British conducted themselves as though the area were exclusively theirs for exploitation, regarding their American rivals with expressions ranging from amusement to contempt. In conference, the leaders usually assumed the hauteur of those dealing with upstarts.

There was, of course, a hard, commercial purpose behind the attitudes as well as the actions of the North West Company men. No trading concern could operate successfully without possessing a monopoly in the area from which furs were to be withdrawn. Not only were fur-bearing animals limited in number, but company agents depended by necessity on the tribes of the region for their supply. No organization could have supported a sufficient number of white trappers to bring in the requisite skins, so an agent's first duty was to persuade the tribesmen to spend their winters following the trap line. This obligation appears to have been difficult enough to fulfill under the most favorable conditions, since the Indians did not always show that fidelity to commercial interests which is supposed to have motivated their employers. War, hunting, whim, and even an occasional baffling indifference to trade goods were problems confronting the company man even in the best of times, and bad weather or scarcity of animals could be ruinous. But where two companies tried to compete, the sum of difficulties was multiplied. Not only had the winter's catch to be divided between them, but each must contend with the other in an attempt to secure the loyalties of Indian trappers. Since each tribe was a separate nation, a company proposing to do business entered into a treaty relationship. In order to give themselves status equal to that assumed by the chiefs with whom they were negotiating, the agents were in the habit of representing themselves as emissaries of their government, a habit somewhat justified by custom and the charters or other forms of legal permission sometimes granted to nationals bound on commercial enterprises. Where a competitive situation existed, the same tribes were asked to enter into contracts with representatives of two nations, each asking for identical rights and privileges. Where a tribe had already entered into a contract with one company, the other, having come late to the field, tried to induce the chiefs to break their agreement. Sometimes the representatives of the concern without a contract attempted to buy the collected furs before they could be delivered.

This was commercial warfare. The established company must fight or withdraw, while the newcomer, by the very act of entering the territory, declared his intention of driving the occupant from the field. In the collecting of furs, no form of competition was acceptable; the only aim was to seize and maintain the position of monopoly made essential by the conditions of the trade.

These matters were well known to the men at Astoria. Astor himself was well acquainted with the difficulties involved as a result of his years of successful operation in the Northwest Territory. Perhaps it was his experience that led him, while still forming his plans for Astoria, to attempt an agreement with the North West Company regarding regions of operation. This precaution, as wise as it was futile, won him nothing but rebuffs. Yet he persisted in his plans, knowing that the area in which he was interested had not been extensively exploited by the British, whose headquarters were in

Canada, or by the Russians, who were located in what is now coastal Alaska. The country from the mouth of the Columbia inland to the river's headwaters was free, but certainly would not remain so for long. This was too tempting a vacuum to remain unfilled.

His choice of site was admirable. From Astoria canoes were paddled far into the hinterland which is now Oregon, Washington, and Idaho. Laden with supplies on their way up the rivers, they were to return from the inland stations carrying cargoes of furs. These were to be taken aboard ocean-going vessels anchored at the post and dispatched with relative ease either to China or to New York. Because of its accessibility by sea and by river alike, the fort was to stand at the watery crossroads between wildest America and the great cities of the world.

Another instance of the care with which Astor designed his undertaking is to be found in the auxiliary projects which were to support the post by providing additional sources of supply as well as to insure a profit by securing varied means of obtaining income. On learning that the Russian posts were supplied only sporadically, he proposed to offer a regular service, using for the purpose ships already required for his own venture. The Hawaiian Islands, he believed, offered not only a market for trade but a supply of laborers. Other possibilities were considered and accepted, until Astoria became not so much a place as a web of actual and potential activity touching such remote points as Canton, St. Petersburg, the Falkland Islands, Alaska, and the Rocky Mountains. But the crucial center of this empire in Astor's conception was the huddle of rude buildings near the mouth of the Columbia. According to the fate of Fort Astoria the empire would live or disappear into the limbo of forgotten projections.

It disappeared. Despite Astor's careful planning and enthusiastic support, the enterprise was overwhelmed by a series

of difficulties too great to be surmounted. Two of the three supply ships were lost, the *Tonquin* being the prey of hostile Indians off Vancouver Island while the *Lark* went down in a
storm off Hawaii. The existence of a state of war enabled the
North West Company to call on the British Navy for assistance in driving out the Americans. The blockade of New
York made the support of Astoria more difficult by virtually
closing the harbor to merchant shipping. Our naval vessels,
far too few in number, were urgently needed elsewhere; consequently, none could be spared for escort duty. Although
Astor's plan had from the beginning been warmly supported
by Jefferson and later won the approval of Madison and Gal-
latin as well, none of the three were ever in a position to lend
actual support. The U.S.S. *Constitution* did escort the *Lark*
for a few hours until the dangerous stretch of water off Sandy
Hook had been safely crossed, but this was the only act of
assistance performed by the government in Astor's behalf.
In contrast, His Majesty's Government placed at the disposal
of the North West Company the sloop-of-war *Racoon*, a vessel of twenty-six guns.

Apart from the difficulties either occasioned by war or in-
herent in the attempt, there is a distinct possibility that the
downfall of Astoria may have been aided by betrayal. Certainly McDougal, the partner most frequently in charge at the
fort, demonstrated a startling eagerness to deal with the agents
of the rival company, as well as a singular ineptness at protect-
ing the interests of his employer. He neither followed the con-
ventional practice of hiding furs and other valuables nor made
the slightest attempt at a military defense, even when Com-
comly, chief of a near-by tribe, offered to drive the British
out for him. Nor did he at any other time display the interest
in supporting the enterprise that might have been expected of
him. Perhaps the Astorians were not surprised when, shortly
after the American flag was hauled down on December 12,

1813, he appeared as a full partner in the North West Company.

Regardless of the cause of its failure, the Astoria venture disappeared, leaving hardly a trace in the broad pattern of a nation's development. Oregon became a part of the United States, but not because a group of fur traders had come from the sea to set up an establishment on the banks of the Columbia. The march was overland, and the lure was not fur but a deep, rich soil. The wagons that rolled across the continent carried stoves, plows, and bedsteads, and beside them plodded people who had come to stay. The beaver were scarce in the streams and the trade itself almost ended by the time that Great Britain and the United States were to establish a mutual boundary far north of the Columbia River. The *voyageur*, the hunter, and the trapper were gone, leaving nothing for remembrance but a few place names, a few routes of travel, and occasional passages of description in the journals of more literate adventures.

I I I

BY A CURIOUS IRONY, the only part of the entire Astoria venture to have a lasting effect was a journey undertaken by a minor partner, a man twenty-seven years old who left the post on a very difficult but not extraordinary mission. Robert Stuart's assignment was to deliver to Astor the dispatches which would serve as an accounting for the partners and employees who had then been working in his behalf for two years. Nor was he the first selected, the duty having been assigned to and unsuccessfully attempted by John Reed, another partner. Out of this combination of circumstance and plain necessity came the opportunity which led to the discovery of the route known as the Oregon Trail.

Stuart's was a discovery in the fullest sense of the term:

he was the first to find and follow a route from the Pacific to St. Louis that could be utilized by wagon trains. Not only Lewis and Clark but Hunt and others had already made their way through the Rockies, but by canoe, on horseback, or afoot. Unable to carry food or supplies in any quantity, they had been forced to rely on hunting for subsistence, a means of support that was precarious even in the unsettled West. Expeditions sometimes came to a standstill while every available man took part in a widespread search for the elusive buffalo, an animal that for all its numbers could disappear as though wiped out by a plague. The Plains Indians had achieved their own solution by surrendering completely to the vagaries of the game they depended on; organizing themselves for mobility, they followed wherever the buffalo chose to wander. To some extent white traders and explorers had been forced to do the same.

Before a more complex society could be established in the West, there had necessarily to be a dependable food supply, for without it people could not remain long enough in one place to develop the detailed patterns of organization required for civilized living. Food meant agriculture, and agriculture required pitchforks, barrels, scythes, and cattle—above all, draft animals and plows. Family groups were required, people trained in the co-operative life of the farm rather than the lore of the plains. Only settlers equipped with farm tools could create the element of stability essential to civilization.

But families and implements could only be transported in wagons, which were themselves a required item of farm equipment. The prime necessity was therefore a roadway through the Rockies, for without it the thousands of white-topped schooners that crawled up the Platte to Fort Laramie and across Wyoming to South Pass could never have reached that climactic point and started the long, rough roll down to the Pacific.

The wagon trains that jolted across the continent in the middle decades of the century followed with little variation the route that Stuart and his men had so stubbornly sought among the misleading waterways of Idaho and western Wyoming in 1812. It was his route, not those of the earlier explorers, which made the green coastal valleys accessible. The "Travelling Memoranda's" account of directions, known geographical points, and structural conformations indicates almost beyond a doubt that he entered South Pass; probably he was the first white man to do so. Certainly he found the route along the Platte, and in so doing came upon the best way to Missouri and the western fringe of civilization. However, it would be a mistake to evaluate Stuart's achievement in terms of prior arrivals. The importance of his journey will be in no way diminished by a discovery that some wandering trapper preceded him at one of these points. What Stuart contributed to the people of the United States was not merely an awareness of new rivers, mountains, and plains, but a device, a means by which they could transfer their families, their tools, and their beliefs to an area that promised to reward them with better lives than the ones they had put behind.

As a wagon trace Stuart's route was long, crooked, rough, and sometimes steep. It crossed treacherous rivers, crawled up pitches slanted so sharply against the sky that the wide-wheeled schooners had to be snaked up one by one and then eased down with back-breaking toil, then leveled out on endless stretches of prairie where the heavy-footed oxen plodded hock-deep in dust. Through mud and sand it twisted, and past the scenes of future quarrels, epidemics, deaths, births, and Indian skirmishes, sometimes to emerge at the beginning of a grim reach without grass or water, mile on mile of sagebrush and choking alkali that must be beaten before men and animals collapsed. Here a broken axle could mean death under a blistering sun, and the small heaps of bones that were to appear beside the deepening ruts would be for some a prophecy as well as a threat.

Yet the route was to prove passable. With the Rocky Mountains no longer a barrier, the way was open for the last great migration, the culmination of the westward movement beginning at Jamestown and Plymouth and ending only when the continent was spanned. With stable populations in the Middle West and on the Pacific Coast, the intervening areas filled rapidly. Out of the wilderness were formed territories which soon became states, and by the end of the nineteenth century the United States was geographically complete.

IV

IMPORTANT TO THE HISTORIAN, the Stuart manuscript is of interest to the student of Washington Irving's works as well. In 1836, Irving published *Astoria*, a book which told the story of Astor's attempt to establish a post near the shores of the Pacific. To aid him he had many records of the enterprise, among them the one he entitled the "Travelling Memoranda." Chapters XII through XX of Volume II are drawn directly from Stuart's account, a circumstance that makes possible an exact comparison between the published version and the original.

The advantage of such a study lies in the changes it reveals, since these may be taken as indicating Irving's conceptions of what literature should be. When looped in the coils of one of his own creations, he was not always as easily read as could be wished; it cannot be stated with certainty that he always knew the direction in which his work was carrying him. But here he was shaping objectively the writing of another, a task that allowed him to bring to bear without prejudice all the aesthetic, moral, or social doctrines applicable. He was under no obligation either to alter the document in hand or to

Robert Stuart

leave it as he found it; the changes to be discovered in the comparison are the expressions not of necessity but of belief.

An example of how a writer may deceive himself and his readers is found in the introduction to *Astoria,* where he wrote that "it occurred to me that a work of this kind might comprise a variety of those curious details, so interesting to me, illustrative of the fur trade; of its remote and adventurous enterprises, and of the various people, and tribes, and castes, and characters, civilized and savage, affected by its operations." If this statement is taken to mean that Irving intended to present a conception true both to the facts in the manuscripts before him and to the tone or attitude of the writers toward their material, he must be considered to have failed in his transcription of the "Travelling Memoranda." However, a comparison of the two versions shows that his real though unprofessed aim was to tell a lively, colorful story, an end which he achieved with distinction. While most of his statements of fact coincide with Stuart's, there are deviations that demonstrate how willingly he took his departure from the words before him. Irving used the facts where they served his purpose; where they did not, he omitted them or substituted the product of his invention.

Three incidents from *Astoria* illustrate his willingness to depart from the material before him. The first of these is the vignette of the "noble animal," an imaginative elaboration of several remarks of Stuart's to the effect that he had bought a horse from an Indian and later reluctantly sold it back because peaceful relationships with the neighboring tribes were of more value than the horse, and that on a different occasion another animal had been stolen by an Indian living lower on the Snake River. Nothing is said in the "Travelling Memoranda" about the quality of the horses, though mention is made of the "extravagant" price paid for one of them.

Out of these instances Irving created his account of a

single magnificent beast "admirably shaped, of free and generous spirit, graceful in movement, and fleet as an antelope." He then skirted the ludicrous by adding, "it was his [Stuart's] intention, if possible, to take the horse to New York, and present him to Mr. Astor."[1] However, rascality supposedly prevented the achievement of this laudable aim. The former owner returned and begged to be allowed to buy the horse back, an offer that was rejected with proper indignation. Thwarted in his attempt to regain the horse legitimately, the Indian returned by night and used theft to achieve his object. In this manner Mr. Astor was, according to Irving, deprived of a mount.

The second of Irving's inventions was a giant Indian chief. Truly a literary character, he had no counterpart in the manuscript and yet was woven very neatly into the fabric of the factual material. He indulged in a brief wrestle with Robert Stuart, led an attack against the group of whites, and made a gesture so very insulting that one of the party was made to exclaim, "Oh, Mr. Stuart . . . only let me have one crack at the infernal rascal, and you may keep all the pay that is due to me." To this plea Irving's Stuart replies, "By heaven, if you fire . . . I'll blow your brains out."[2] By the time this bit of dramatic dialog is over, the picturesque chief has ridden out of range and out of the book, leaving Irving to return to more factual matter.

The third invention is an incident that supposedly happened to Crooks, an actual member of Stuart's party. Irving's account states that Crooks wandered away from camp without his gun, a piece of carelessness described as a "rare circumstance." While standing on a hill, he observed objects which soon became visible as a grizzly and her two cubs. Crooks

---

[1] Washington Irving, *Astoria*, Gift Edition (New York, G. P. Putnam's Sons, 1901), II, 162.
[2] *Ibid.*, 184.

prudently lay down to conceal himself, watching the movements of the animals with "intense anxiety" and no doubt meditating on the folly of absent-mindedness. Fortunately the mother changed her course, and "Mr. Crooks made all haste back to camp, rejoicing at his escape, and determining never to stir out again without his rifle."[3]

As the three inventions indicate, Irving showed a persistent desire to speed up the action of the account. The story of the "noble animal" demonstrates his method of making *Astoria* more colorful than the original by substituting the unusual for the ordinary, using the element of strangeness to catch his reader's attention. The description of action served the same end. Just as the physical eye is caught by the unusual outline, the brilliant color, or the moving object, the eye of the imagination focuses at once on the unusual in the literary scene. This tendency Irving steadily utilized, adding, omitting, and rearranging to achieve the effect of visual appeal which he recognized as an important element in the storyteller's art.

Equally important is the attitude taken by the author toward the characters and incidents he describes. Are they to appear to him, and subsequently to his reader, as comic, tragic, or light-heartedly romantic? Where will he and his audience stand in order to view them? What tone shall he establish for his tale?

For Irving, the answer was gallantry. Stuart and his men were seen as individuals deliberately pitting themselves against the wilderness in order to demonstrate that they could conform to a code of chivalric conduct in the face of difficulties. They would win if possible, but victory must be achieved within the rules or it would lose its savor. The final triumph was to be over the baser impulses: the urge to flee, the desire to gain advantage through deceit, the willingness to placate. Like ambitious squires they exposed themselves

[3] *Ibid.*, 229.

to danger hoping to prove to their own satisfaction and to the world's that they were worthy of esteem.

The tone of the "Travelling Memoranda" contrasts sharply with that of *Astoria*. Stuart was a man bent on carrying out his duty no matter what it might be, an employee whose professional obligation was to John Jacob Astor and the Pacific Fur Company. The code that guided him was that of justice reinforced by the teachings of the Calvinist religion, not a gentlemanly conception of chivalric behavior. His character had been tried before he left Astoria; no doubt he would have been amused by the thought of deliberately seeking difficulties. In marked contrast to Irving's character of the same name, Stuart did not hesitate to placate wherever a mild manner seemed more likely to win him through, or to change his route in an attempt to avoid trouble entirely. Having nothing to prove to himself, he was capable of subordinating his ego to the task at hand, his restraints being not an assumed code of behavior, but his own mature understanding of loyalty, justice, and morality.

He regarded the events described in his manuscript with complete seriousness, since many had been threats to the lives of seven men. With the possibility that everything might be lost, he had struggled eternally onward. Even without the stimulus of duty there would have been nothing else to do, for with only a few scraps of dried meat between the party and starvation, it was move or die. The singular aspect of Stuart's achievement does not lie in the instinct that prompted him to stay on his feet, but in the combination of intellectual and spiritual qualities which kept him always in command of himself and his situation, even when attacked simultaneously by bitter fatigue, debilitating hunger, and prospects so dismaying as to appear almost hopeless. He was determined to stay alive, and without being degraded as a man.

It is in the expression of this attitude that his version

differs most basically from Irving's. The victory here was won in the adult's defensive battle against the forces that would degrade him in his own eyes, not in the youthful manhood test to which the characters in *Astoria* were submitted.

By rejecting the tone of the original, Irving demonstrated his distaste for the moral struggle as well as his predilection for that kind of adventure which evoked the picturesque in posture, setting, and deed. Once again the author of *The Sketch-Book* had his pencil in hand, but on this occasion he appears to have used it as a means of defending himself against the type of theme that some of his contemporaries were beginning to make known. What the comparison of the two works shows is not so much the adherence to a familiar mode as the refusal to enter upon the complexities of the inner nature. Had he been in the slightest disposed to try it, the "Travelling Memoranda" would have given him every opportunity to attempt the portrayal of man's conflict with the invisible. Instead, he forcibly converted it into a tale of derring-do.

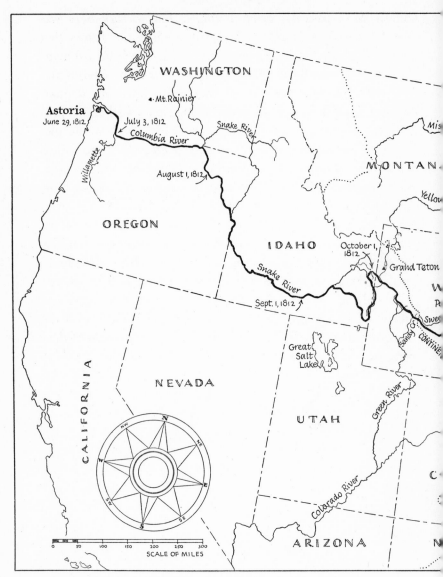

The route followed by Robert Stuart and his party from Fort Astoria to St. Louis, June 29, 1812–April 30, 1813, shown in relation to present state boundaries. While no attempt has

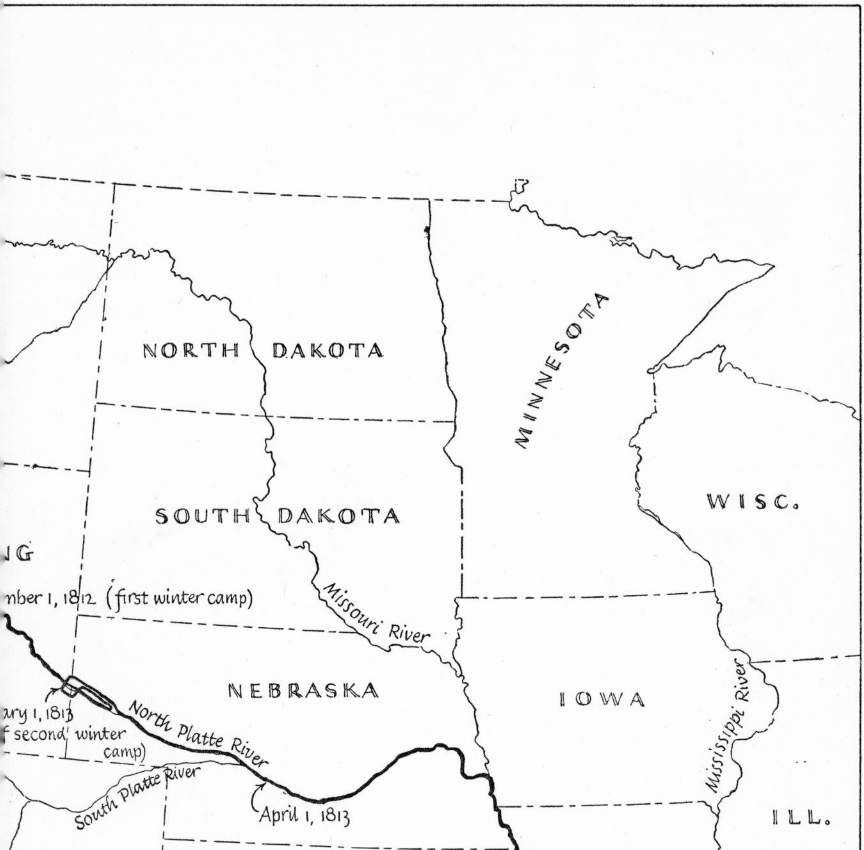
NORTH DAKOTA
SOUTH DAKOTA
MINNESOTA
WISC.
NEBRASKA
IOWA
ILL.
KANSAS
MISSOURI
OKLAHOMA
XICO
DO
IG
nber 1, 1812 (first winter camp)
Missouri River
North Platte River
South Platte River
April 1, 1813
Mississippi River
Missouri River
St. Louis
April 30, 1813

been made to indicate the camping sites of the party in terms of subsequent towns and cities, the places and dates given are roughly at thirty-day intervals to show the rate of progress.

*Retour de l'embouchure de la Columbia
jusques au Missouri
par [Stuart] & six personnes*

*Return from the mouth of the Columbia
to the Missouri
by [Stuart] and six men*

This inscription may have been added to the manuscript by one
of the editors who prepared it for publication in Paris in 1821.

[June 1812]

In the afternoon of monday the 29t June 1812,[1] we sailed from Astoria, under a salute of cannon from the Fort; Messrs. Hunt, McDougall, Ehnenger, and Capt. Soule, of the Ship Beaver, accompanied us as far as Tongue Point, where we found two Barges and ten canoes, which had set out from the establishment this morning, destined for the interior parts of the country above the forks of the Columbia—Messrs. Mc-Kenzie, D. Stuart, and Clarke had charge of the two Boats and nine canoes, with seven clerks, thirty-two Canadians, and twelve Sandwich Islanders under their command.—the other is intended for the conveyance of Messrs. Crooks, & McClellan, Benjamin Jones, John Day, Andre Vallee, François Leclerc (engagés), and myself, with the necessaries for the procecution of this voyage.—It being late, and some preparations necessary, we agreed to pass the night here, which is four miles above Astoria and nineteen from Cape Disappointment.—

Fort Clatsop, the residence of Capts. Lewis & Clark while in this country, is now in ruins, and distant about seven miles in a south east direction, it was very disagreeably situ-

[1] In general, the spelling, punctuation, and grammar of the original have been retained. Here and there an obvious slip of the hand has been corrected, a truly puzzling point of punctuation altered. The aim has been to preserve the character of Stuart's writing, as far as that may be done without raising difficulties for the reader.

ated, being surrounded with swamps and quagmires, but the immense number of Elk & wild Fowl, which resort thither in winter for feed, more than compensates for that inconvenience.—The Columbia is six miles wide at our *fort*, crossing from thence to point Chinook, but both above and below it is nearly twice as much.—It would be in vain to attempt giving a description of our establishment in its present unfinished state; I will therefore content myself by observing that it is delightfully situated on the South east extremity of Point George, which is a commanding, as well as in every other respect a commodious station, having an excellent harbour within fifty yards of the shore for vessels not exceeding two hundred tons.—our present fortification in place of being 120 square yards in extent, as was at first projected, is only about 75 feet by 80, it is well stockaded with pickets 17 feet long and 18 inches diameter, having two strong Bastions, at opposite angles, so as to rake two sides each; inside are a framed store, two stories high, 60 feet by 20, with good cellars and a powder magazine.—a dwelling house, one story high, & 60 feet by 25.—a Black Smith's shop, and a large shade for carpenters, Coopers, &ct.; the ensuing winter about twenty men are to be employed in extending the Fortification, and 30 are now engaged in preparing a frame for a dwelling house, to be two stories high, & 60 by 30 feet, which, with another Store and kitchen, shall be the principal additions made to the present buildings.—

The Chinooks and Clatsops are the only Tribes in the immediate vicinity, the former can bring 214 and the latter 180 fighting men into the field.—About 40 miles to the Northward, along the Coast, live the Chi-hee-leesh, 234 men, and about the same distance to the southward are the Callemax, in number 200; these four nations generally come directly to the establishment, with what Furs &ct. they have to trade, which for the most part consist, of Sea Otter, Beaver, River

Otter, Bear Skins, dressed Elk skins, Muskrats, Salmon, and Roots—but the Chinooks are more especially the intermediate traders between the whites and inland Tribes, particularly those to the northward.—Deer, and a few Bear, are to be found in the neighborhood of our establishment, but Elk is almost the only Animal which may be called an inhabitant of the country immediately on the Coast, and untill the brushwood ceases to grow, will very probably remain so; the country is likewise so remarkably broken, and heavily timbered, that it is seldom possible to distinguish an object more than 100 yards, which when added to an impenetrable undergrowth affords such a secure retreat that the utmost efforts of the hunter are seldom crowned with success, besides from the middle of October to that of March, no man in the woods can possibly keep his Arms in order, in consequence of the unceasing rains which fall during these five months.—The whole tract of country along the Coast is remarkably rugged and mountainous, and in my opinion, the clouds collected on these mountains, uniting with those which come off the ocean, must occasion this sucession of heavy rains, which is frequently accompanied by tremendous thunder & lightning, the remainder of the year (if an almost total want of the descending fluid may be so called) possesses the best and most agreeable weather imaginable.—The dews are abundant throughout this whole country, in the Spring, Summer, and Autumnal nights, and in a great measure supply the want of rain during these seasons, altho' the atmosphere is then loaded with humidity, its wholesomeness is not in the least injured thereby, for both natives and whites sleep in the open air with perfect security. —Fogs are very common along and in the vicinity of the Coast, especially in the spring and Autumn, however these continue generally but a few hours in the morning, and as they consist only of watery particles, are not, like ours, prejudicial to the health of the inhabitants, or (from appearances) to vegitation—the S. & S. East winds usually bring rain, and the North to S. West, a clear sky; these serve as infalliable indications to the aborigines who thereby presume to prognosticate the state of the weather.—From the Coast to the neighborhood of the Cordilleras, or Rocky Mountains, the quantity of snow that falls in the winter is very trifling, it usually melts while falling, and it is uncommon to have it remain on the ground more than 2 or 3 days, except on the highest summits of the mountains, which are constantly covered with snow, are distinguishable at a great distance by their whiteness, which occasions their forming a very singular, pleasing appearance.—

The mild temperature which this tract of country almost always enjoys must depend in great measure upon the succession of winds from the Pacific Ocean, which extend from Latitude 20 to at least 50 North; their effect is equally agreeable in the summer, for they cool the air so much that, in the shade, no one is ever incommoded with perspiration: and the dress of the inhabitants is the same in summer as in Winter.—

The difference in the vegitation of the maratime and interior countries depends less upon the inequality of the climate than that of their respective soils; that upon the Coast is generally poor ground, of a brown colour, inclining to red, it is brittle, and in some parts clayey, and mingled with gravel —In the interior, or rather in the vallies of the Rocky Mountains, the soil is generally of a blackish colour, but in some places yellow, and frequently mixed with marll and marine substances in a state of decomposition; this quality of the soil is continued to a considerable depth, as is discernable in the ravines and beds of rivers.—The vegitation in these vallies is much more vigerous and exuberant than near the coast.— The principal trees, that came within the compass of my perambulations, are the Hemlock, spruce, white and red Cedar (all of which grow to an enormous size), and incredible as it may appear, we found some of them 7 & 9 fathoms in circumference, and 250 to 300 feet long; there are likewise white oak, white and swamp ash, Cottonwood, Willow, and a few Walnut.—of aromatic shrubs, and other undergrowth, there is an endless variety, as also of Berries, such as Gooseberries, Strawberries, Raspberries (of two kinds, red and yellow, and very large, having an exceeding fine flavour), Whortleberries, Cranberries, Juniper berries, Serviceberries, Blue or Blacberries, Currants, Sloes, Wild or Choke Cherries &ct.—Climbing plants or creepers are found in great abundance in all the thickets, among others is a species of vine that deserves to be noticed; its flowers, each of which is composed of six petals or leaves, about 3 inches in length, are of the most beautiful crimson, spotted within with white; its leaves are disposed by threes, of a handsome green and an oval shape, this plant climbs upon the trees like the ivy, but without attaching itself to them; when it reaches the top of a tree, it descends from it perpendicularly, and as it continues to grow, extends from tree to tree, untill at length it exhibits some resemblance to the rigging of a Ship, it is much tougher and more flexible than Willow, and can be procured from 50 to 100 fathoms in length; the Indians manufacture baskets of it, which are of so close a texture as to hold water, and are employed for many domestic purposes.—The principal quadrupids I have seen, are the Moose Deer, or Elk, the Stag, the fallow Deer, Hart, black and grizzly Bear, Antelope, Ibex, Beaver, Sea and River Otter, Muskrats, Foxes, Wolves, a few Panthers &ct.[2]—Horses and Dogs are the only domestic animals in possession of the natives.—

The country abounds with an infinity of both aquatic and land Birds, particularly the Swan, Wild Goose, Brant, Ducks

[2] The vine here described I have not been able to identify. Moose, elk, Columbian black-tailed deer, mule deer, and white-tailed deer lived in the area. Stuart's ibex appear to have been mountain sheep.

of almost every description, Pelicans, Herons, Gulls, Snipe, Curlews, Eagles, Vultures, Crows, Ravens, Magpies, Woodpeckers, Wild Pigeons, Partridges, Grouce, Pheasant, and a very numerous collection of singing Birds.—

The Rivers are remarkably well stocked with Salmon, Sturgeon, Trout, Chub, Conger, and a variety of fresh water smelt, which are excellent of their kind.—

There are very few reptiles in the Country, and the only dangerously venemous ones are the Rattle-Snake and a kind of Serpent,[3] which is striped with black, yellow, and white, sometimes mixed with brown, the largest I have seen of eother did not exceed 4 feet in length; in the swamps a great many Snakes may be found, but are all harmless; there are also Frogs, Toads. Land Turtles, and a kind of Lizard, which lives usually under ground in the plains, their length exclusive of the tail is nine or ten inches, and three inches in circumference, the head is triangular, covered with small square scales, the upper part of the body is covered with small scales, green, yellow, black and blue; the feet have each five toes, furnished with strong nails; the tail is round, and of the same length and colour as the body;—[4]

The Coast near the mouth of the River, produces a few Sea Otter, and some scattering Beaver, which the Natives, both from inexperience and indolence, seem as yet little inclined to reduce in number, altho' their sole dependence for sustenance is upon Fish, Roots, and what few Animals they can kill.—few Salmon are caught before the latter end of May, but from that till the middle of August, they can be got in great plenty, and are by far the finest fish I ever beheld;

[3] The "Serpent" was either a rattlesnake or a harmless reptile of unknown variety.

[4] There are lizards vaguely similar in the Columbia drainage. Here as elsewhere, Stuart's descriptions of animal life illustrate the difficulties encountered by the sharp-eyed but untrained observer who must delineate a number of species he has never before encountered.

they are mostly caught in shallow water, by scenes made of nettles.—from August untill December is the season for *Dog-tooth Salmon*, a very inferior species of that fish, and so named by us from their having a double row of teeth, exceedingly sharp and at least half an inch long; they are generally killed with the Spear, in small rivulets, smoked, and laid by as store for the dreary months of January and February, after which Sturgeon and Uth-le-chan may be taken in great numbers, the former sometimes by the Spear, but more generally by the hook and line; and the latter by the scoop net.—The Uthle-chan is about six inches long, and somewhat similar to our smelt, is a very delicious little fish, and so fat as to burn like a candle, and are often used for that purpose by the natives.—

The Religion or rather enthusiastic superstition of these people I have not sufficient opportunity, or knowledge of their language, to investigate fully, and notwithstanding my making the strictest enquiries, all I could collect was that they represent the supreme being, as an immense Bird, inhabiting the Sun (called by them Uth-lath-Gla-gla), being a benevolent spirit, and omnipotent,—to him they attribute the creation, and suppose him capable of assuming any shape or appearance at pleasure, but upon extraordinary occurances, he is believed to take the likeness aforesaid, occasionally ranging through the aerial regions, and in his wrath hurling down Thunder & lightning upon us guilty Mortals; to him they offer annual sacrifices, of their first Salmon, Venison &ct. &ct.—A particular being is ascribed to the fire, of whom they are in perpetual dread, and constantly offer sacrifices, supposing him equally possessed of the power of good and evil: they are very desirous of being patronised by this gentleman, for it is he alone who has the power of interceding with their winged protector, and procure them all desirable things, such as male children, a plentiful fishing, an abundance of game, with comforts and riches of every description.—

When any of their chief personages is supposed to be on his death bed, or any way in imminent danger of his life, all the Literati of the Nation are immediately convened, the High Priest and Physician, or *medicine Man,* brings and consults each his deity (i.e., the benevolent, or spirit of the air, and that of the Fire), which are made of wood and ingeniously carved, with a number of Beaver's teeth, Bear and Eagles claws suspended from them; they are capriciously formed, in shape of a Horse, Bear, Deer, Beaver, Swan, Fish &ct.: Those Idols, with their possessors, are placed in a remote corner of the Lodge for the purpose of consultation, but should they not agree regarding the patients malady, the owners, who are mostly always competitors for fame, power, and influence, beat them violently against each other, untill a tooth or claw falls of[f] one, which is always taken as a full proof of his confutation, consequently the advice, and prescriptions, of the other are implicitly attended to; should the sick person recover, a sacrifice is immediately made to the revered deity, and his adherent is liberally rewarded, but should he on the contrary make his exit, no offering or compensation is given, and the failure is entirely attributed to the displeasure of the offended deity.—A day or two after his death, a few of the nearest relatives carry off the corpse, which, with his most valuable moveables, they deposit in a canoe prepared for the purpose and neatly covered with handsome matts, made of straw, they then lay it on a scaffold, or suspend it between two trees, in a retired part of the woods; all the deceased's well wishers cut of[f] their hair in token of grief, and for several days, neither eat nor drink, but mope about the village, howling and lamenting the departed; when the season of mourning is over (which generally lasts about one Month), a division of the slaves and other property takes place agreeably to the defuncts request on his death bed.—

Their manner of courtship and marriage is somewhat

Indian Canoe, The Dalles

singular; *when a fair one has the good fortune to kindle a
flame in the bosom of a hero,* he watches for a private conference, and if favorably received, repairs soon after to her
Father's lodge, with a considerable present, which he care-
lessly throws down at the old Gentleman's feet, then his intention is disclosed, generally by a friend he prefers on this
important occasion; the Sire then enquires whether the pro-
posal is agreeable to his daughter, and on being answered in
the affirmative, demands so many slaves, Horses, Canoes, &ct.
according to her beauty and accomplishments, and promises a
certain return on her going into house-keeping; preliminaries
thus settled, the remainder of the day is devoted to festivity
and mirth,—at a late hour the party breaks up, and all retire
to rest, except the lover, who steals to her Ladyship's couch,
where he remains untill morning, when, if they are satisfied
with each other's company, the match is finally settled; but
should either be inclined to retract, they are at liberty so to
do, as the present the lover has made his intended Father-in-
law is thought a full equivalent for this breach in the maid's
virtue or reputation.—Both sexes seem incapable of forming
any tender attachment, the women are very inconstant to their
husbands, the worst of disorders is deeply rooted among them,
having been first introduced by some of our country-men,
probably from the Sandwich Islands, where it has been known,
time immemorial, the effects however are not so destructive
as might be expected.—

Poligamy is not only allowed, but considered honorable,
and the greater number of wives a man can maintain, the more
power & influence has he in the Nation.—The first wife is always respected as the real and legitimate one by all the others,
who are called secondary wives; she has the management of
all domestic concerns and regulates the interior of the house;
the husband has sometimes much to do to keep harmony among
so many women, who are not a little inclined to jealousy, the

usual manner is, each night at supper, to make known his choice of her, who is to have the honor of sharing his bed, by directing her to prepare it.—

The chieftainship is not hereditary, but he who exceeds in the number of his wives, male children, and slaves, is elected.—

Their system of criminal jurisprudence, in a particular manner, is very imperfect: the offences that are deemed deserving of capital punishments are treachery, intentional homicide, and the robbery of any valuable article, nevertheless those found guilty of homicide can most generally screen themselves from punishment by a composition with the relatives of the murdered,—but should the assassin be inclined to make no reparation or concession, the injured family often assume the right of pursuing and punishing him, or some of his kindred, considering themselves under the most sacred obligations of supporting, even by force, the rights of their relations—

Husbands and Fathers are not subject to any punishment for killing their wives or children, as they are declared by their laws to be natural masters of their lives.—but most generally the power of deciding controversies and of punishing offences is intrusted to the chiefs—they being considered by the lower order as omniscient, and having an indisputable right to those privileges, however it cannot be supposed that a rugged proprietor of the forest or Rocks, unprincipled and unenlightened, can be a nice resolver of entangled claim, or very exact in proportioning punishments to offenses, but generally the more he indulges his own will, the more he holds his subjects in dependence, therefore innocence and forbearance, without the favor of the Chief, confer no security, and crimes however atrocious involve no danger when the judge is resolute to acquit.—

Their arms are principally Bows and Arrows, Iron and

bone Bludgeons, with a few muskets, which they are extremely fond of, and so much is their effect dreaded by the surrounding tribes (who have few or none) that a dosen on either side are sufficient to decide their most obstinate conflicts—when a quarrel arises between two tribes, a day and place are appointed, where the affair is settled in a *pitched battle,* which is their universal mode of warfare; they generally prefer the banks of a rivulet for the field of action, and post the adverse parties on either side of the stream; the number killed and wounded never exceed half a dosen, and should an equal number of each party fall, the war is ended, but otherwise the conquerors must make an equivalent compensation, in slaves, &ct., else hostilities are renewed on a future day; they seldom make prisoners, but when this is the case, they are always well treated and never reduced to slavery; these poor creatures are procured from the interior Tribes, who are of savage nations, their military power is an undiciplined rabble, unfit to content with ⅕ their number of Whites: They like the others seldom shed much blood in their engagements, and sometimes battles are fought which last 2 or 3 days, yet altho' 5 or 600 men may be engaged on each side, and the conflict terminated in a complete rout, the whole loss is seldom more than 12 or 15 killed and wounded,—predatory excursions are the favorite war like exploits of these people; consequently, many such plundering parties are formed who make frequent incursions on their enemies, and sometimes upon their friendly neighbors, they seldom exceed 50 or 60 in number, but when fortunate enough to fall on a small band, they massacre all the men, and carry away the women and children as slaves, the rest of their plunder is carried off on horses, each man being provided with two or three of these animals on all such expeditions.—

There is perhaps no race of people in the world (for that they are of the same origin I have little doubt) who can exhibit a greater variety, with regard to size and appearance, than those of the tract we traverse.—The affluent (as they may be termed) whose good fortune has placed them among the Buffalo plains, on the east side of the mountains, are generally from 5 feet 8 to 6 feet 2 inches in stature, well proportioned, extremely strong and active—while the indigent inhabitants of the western side are in general below the middle size, indolent, and of a very unhealthy complexion, evidently stunted by the badness of their food and the want of proper clothing; it is however very uncommon to find a crooked or deformed person among them, not from their pursuing, as some have maintained, the cruel custom of destroying such unfortunate children, but, in my belief, because they leave to nature the care of forming them, without obstructing her operations by the improper application of bandages, stays, corsets &ct. &ct.

They have very round faces, with small animated eyes, a broad flat nose, a handsome mouth, even and white teeth, well shaped legs and small flat feet.—In their infancy the crown and forehead are flatened, by means of a small piece of board, shaped and tied on for that purpose; this in their opinion is a great acquisition to personal beauty, consequently whoever has the broadest and flatest head is esteemed by far the handsomest person.—They have scarce any beard, and it is seldom the smallest hair is to be discerned on their faces; from the care they take to pluck out the little that appears, they esteem it very uncooth and impolite to have a beard, calling the whites by way of reproach the long beards; the same attention is paid to removing it from their bodies, where its growth is more abundant; that of their head is thick and black, but rather coarse; they allow it to grow to a great length, sometimes wearing it pleated, and sometimes fancifully wound round the head in tresses: of this they are as proud & careful as they are averse to beards, nor could a greater affront be offered them, than to cut it off.—Those whose lot it is to inhabit the interior country depend chiefly on hunting, consequently lead a roving life through the plains, without any stationary habitation, whereas those who live near the sea subsist, I may say entirely, on Fish, and dwell in large scattering villages on the banks of the principal water courses: their lodges are constructed of cedar boards, a little sunk in the ground, and leaning against strong poles set erect, with cross spars which serve likewise as a support to the roof; these dwellings are generally large enough for the accommodation of 3 or 4 families, have a door in the gable end, made of a square piece of board or framed seal skin, a fire place (or places) in the middle, a hole over it in the roof of the house, which serves at once for the discharge of the smoke and the admission of light—the sides are partitioned off, for sitting and sleeping places, and covered with neat grass mats: the principal houses have a small apartment attached to them, which serves as a vapor bath, to prepare which stones must be heated and placed in a large hole, dug in the middle of the bath, or sweating house, where the heat may be encreased to any degree by the steam of the water which is poured on them.—

They pass a great portion of their lives in revelry, and amusement, music, dancing, and play form their customary diversions; as to the first, it scarcely deserves the name, both from the defficiency of their instruments; and their manner of singing has something in it harsh & disagreeable to the ear, their songs being almost all extempore, on any triffeling object that strikes the imagination; they have several kinds of dancing, some of which are lively, pleasing and possess some variety; the women are rarely permitted to dance with the men, but form their companies a part, and dance to the sound of the same instrument and song.—

Their games are numerous, and for the most part ingenious, and they sometimes indulge in play, to very great excess, indeed there have been instances of their losing every-

39

thing they possessed in the world, even their Women, Children and Lodges.—They are notorious thieves, and he who is so dextrous as on all occasions to elude detection is much applauded, acquires great celebrity and popularity; but the wretch who is unfortunate enough to be discovered is severely punished, and sometimes loses an ear &ct., which is thought so disgraceful as to reduce him to a level with the women, and disqualifies him ever after from becoming a warrior; some whose family have influence may be indulged with the privilege of being mogsan carrier to a war party.—

Their general mode of hunting Elk and Deer is with the Bow and Arrow, very few possessing or knowing the use of Fire Arms; they frequently go in large parties, surround the game while grazing in a favorable place, such as a small prairie or meadow, environed by wood; they plant themselves in the different avenues or paths leading to this spot, then set in their dogs, which throws the affrighted animals in such confusion as to scatter in every direction, thereby giving the most, or all, a chance of exercising their skill, for let the consternation of these poor creatures be ever so great, they can only escape by those leading paths.—Some of the best warriors shoot an arrow with such force as to send it thro' an Elk or Buffalo at the distance of 15 or 20 paces.—On certain occasions they use darts, which are adapted with the greatest judgement to the different objects of the chase; for animals, a simple barbed point: for birds, they have them with three points of light bone, spread and barbed; for Seals & sea otter, they use a false point, inserted in a socket at the end of the dart, which parts on the least effort of the animal to dive, remaining in its body: a string of considerable length is fastened to this barbed point, and twisted round the wooden part of the dart; this serves as a float to direct them to the animal, which, having the stick to drag after it, soon tires and becomes an easy prey; (it however requires skill to humour it, perhaps equal to our angling.)—The boards used in throwing these darts are very judiciously fixed, in semblance of a *gutter*, which enables the natives to cast them with great exactness to a considerable distance.—

Their Canoes for the most part are made of Cedar, and altho' possessed of no other instrument than a small chisel, it would be in vain for any White (with every tool he could wish) to set up a competition with them in this art; if perfect symmetry, smoothness, and proportion constitute beauty, they surpass anything I ever beheld: I have seen some of them as transparent as oiled paper, thro' which you could trace every formation of the inside; and the natives of this river & its vicinity are the most expert paddle men any of us had ever seen; two or three of these fellows, in a small canoe, can with perfect security navigate in the most boisterous weather, for no sooner does their canoe fill or upset than they spring into the water (more like amphibious animals than human beings), right, and empty her, when with the greatest composure they again get in, and proceed.—The men never wear any other garment than a small robe, made of Deer or musk-rat-skins, thrown loosly over the shoulders; and the Women have no other addition than a fringe of cedar bark tied round the waist and reaching about two inches below the knees.—There are no two tribes who speak the same tongue, but most generally, each nation understands the tongue of the nearest neighbours on either side, so that each horde may be said to comprehend three different languages.—

They possess their present lands and situation from time immemorial.—They are never troubled with epidemic or contagious diseases, except the small-pox, which, from nation to nation, has found its way across the Rocky mountains, and sometimes its effects are so calamitous as to carry off three fourths of those who have the misfortune to be attacked therewith.—Their method of life neither secures them perpetual health nor exposes them to any particular diseases; it is generally supposed that life is longer in places where there are few opportunities of luxury, but I found few or no instances among them of extraordinary longivety, *an indian grows old over his smoked salmon, just like a citizen over a turtle feast:* instances of long life are often related here, which (it appears to me) those who hear them are more willing to credit than to examine.—

They informed us that Capt. Gray of the Ship Columbia, from Boston, was the first White who entered the River;[5] on the vessels first appearance in the offing, they were very much surprised and alarmed, but after her entering and anchoring in the river, they were all seized with such consternation as to abandon their village, leaving only a few old people who could not follow; some imagined that the ship must be some overgrown monster come to devour them, while others supposed her to be a floating island inhabited by cannibals, sent by the great spirit to destroy them and ravage their country &ct. &ct. however a Boats crew soon went ashore, who by their mild behavior, and distributing a few trinkets, succeeded in assuring the old people of their friendly intentions, which they soon found means to communicate to the fugitives, thus a friendly intercourse was immediately entered into, which has never since been interrupted.—   .

Tuesday 30th   At the dawn of day every man was at his post, and the canoes loaded soon after; a few minutes only were spent in mutual wishes of good health and prosperity between the gentlemen who accompanied us and those of our party, when we embarked and proceeded across shallow-bay—At 2 P.M. passed the Cath-lamet village, containing 94 warriors; and on the opposite side of the river, the Waak-i-cums of 16,

[5] On May 11, 1792.

these last and the Chinooks were originally the same, but on account of a dispute (about two generations back) between the then chief and his brother, the latter separated himself from the nation, and settled where they at present live; his descendants, out of respect to his memory, call themselves after his name: having come about 15 miles, we stopped for the night, on a small rising ground,[6] on the south side,—The natives brought salmon, and a few Beaver-skins to trade.

[6] Two miles northeast of present Brownsmead, Oregon.

[July 1812]

Wednesday 1st. *July*—We imbarked soon after daylight appeared, and experienced a greater degree of rapidity in the current than we had any idea of: the river has fallen very considerably, but not as yet sufficiently to admit of our encamping in the bottoms, indeed from hill to hill the country has no very different appearance from an immense swamp, our days marches are therefore very irregular, being either compelled to stop often at an early hour, or sleep in our boats, without the possibility of finding a sufficiency of land wherein to kindle a fire for culinary purposes.—About two hours before sun set, we reached the establishment made by Capt. Winship of Boston, in the spring of 1810; it is situate on a beautiful high bank on the south side,[1] and enchantingly diversified, with white Oaks, Ash, Cottonwood and Alder, but of rather a diminutive size; here he intended leaving a Mr. Washington, with a party of men, but whether with view of making a permanent settlement or merely for trading with the Indians until his return from the coast, the natives were unable to tell; the water however rose so high as to inundate a house he had already constructed, when a dispute arose between him and the Chilwits, by his putting several of them in irons on the

[1] Three miles north-northwest of the site of Quincy, Oregon.

44

supposition that they were Chee-hee-lish, who had some time previous cut off a schooner belonging to the Russian establishment of New Archangle, by the Governor of which place he was employed to secure any of the banditti who committed this horrid act; the Chilwits made formidable preparations, by engaging auxilliaries &ct. for the release of their relations by force, which coming to the captain's knowledge, as well as the error he had been guilty of, the captives were set free, every person embarked, and left the Columbia without loss of time. —Between the hour we stopped here and dusk, evident symptoms of derangement made their appearance in John Day (one of my hunters), who for a day or two previous seemed as if restless and unwell, but now uttered the most incoherent, absurd and unconnected sentences; several spoke to him, but little satisfaction was obtained, and he went to bed gloomy and churlish.—3 miles below this spot live the Chilwitz, a nation about 200 men; their lands produce a good many Beaver, and Wapatoes in abundance; this root is considerably smaller, but in every other respect bears a strong resemblance to our Potatoe, they are found in marshes and require great labour in extraction.—Here are the best and almost only fisheries of Uthlechans and Sturgeon; the former they take in immense numbers by the operation of the scoop net, from the middle of March till the beginning of May, and the latter principally by the hook and line, during the Spring and Fall seasons; their most common length is about six feet, but some are only four, while others arrive at the enormous length of nine to ten; this neighborhood is also by far the greatest place of resort, in the spring and autumn, for Swan, Geese, and Ducks, for the procuring of which we had a clerk and some men stationed at the Chilwit's village, who, combining that with the fishery, procured us a plentiful subsistence during the last season.—Our distance to day is 22 miles.—

Thursday 2d—At an early hour we set off again, with a fair wind, and at 10 A.M. reached the Cow-lit-sic, a river 200 yards wide, which last winter I navigated with six men for 260 miles, partly for deminishing the number of mouths at the Fort, and partly to explore the interior and trade with the natives: for the first 50 miles, the face of the country evinces your being still in the vicinity of the great river, but from thence to the extreme of my discovery, beautiful high prairies make their appearance, occasionally interspersed with a few Oaks, Walnut, Pines &ct., and are the feeding grounds of a good many Elk, Bear and Deer.—This river takes its rise in mount Rainier, at a small distance from the straits of Juan De Fuca, runs southwardly, is very rapid, and navigable only for 190 miles: Beaver are tolerably plenty and of a good quality; but from my being able to collect no more than 260 skins, among the Le-cow-lit-sic nation of 250 Men, am led to believe them totally ignorant of the mode of taking them.—These people are peaceably inclined, and not so thievishly disposed as those on the coast, but their demeanor is somewhat haughty and insolent.—By sun set we got to Puget's (or Gass' Deer?) Island,[2] where we encamped, it is considerably elevated, but overflows in great freshes, otherwise it would be an excellent place for a permanent settlement.—During the evening John Day's disorder became very alarming, and several times he attempted getting possession of some of our Arms, with the intention of committing suicide, but finding all his attempts fruitless, he at length feigned great remorse, and appeared to feel sencibly the enormity of the crime he premeditated; this change entirely lulled our suspicions, which enabled him (a little before day light) to possess himself of a pair of loaded Pistols, which he pointed at his head and fired, but fortunately too high to take effect; he was instantly secured, and placed

[2] Deer Island.

under a guard in one of the Boats, where I intend to keep him untill we can determine what may be most advisable to be done with him.—To day's march was 25 miles.—

Friday 3*d* By day break we were again in the Boats, our route was south along the Island, to the entrance of the first channel of that large and beautiful stream, called by the Indians Wallamat,[3] by Lewis & Clarke Multnomah, and by Mr. Donald McKenzie, who lately explored it for 500 miles, McKay's River; we then crossed to the Cath-la-pootle Island, where, finding that John Days insanity amounted to real madness, I agreed with some Indians of the Cathlapootle nation (for a few articles) to carry him back to the Fort, as he had become not only an entirely useless member of the expedition, but kept us continually in alarm for his own safety and that of some individuals, against whom he evidently had some evil design,—It was also the opinion of all the gentlemen that it would be highly imprudent to suffer him to proceed any farther, for in a moment when not sufficiently watched, he might enbroil us with the natives, who on all occasions he reviled by the appelations of Rascals, Robbers &ct. &ct. he was completely disarmed before embarking with the chief, who I knew well, and have every confidence in his conducting him back in safety.—

This first branch of the Wallamat is 200 yards wide: at its entrance live the Cathlakamaps about 120 strong, and directly opposite the Cathlapootles of 180.—Immediately above, on Long Island, are the Cathlanaminimins, once a very powerful tribe, but now reduced by the small pox to about 60 men; the upper end of the island (which is 10 miles long) is inhabited by the Mathlanobes, 130 strong, who with those other

[3] Willamette River.

tribes possess a good many Beaver and dressed Elk Skins.—
The main body of the river, which here joins the Columbia in
a northerly direction, is 500 yards from bank to bank; at the
distance of 45 miles above the junction, it is contracted to
about 300 feet in width, where the water rushes over a perpendicular ledge of smooth rock 30 feet high—it soon after
expands to nearly the same breadth as below the Falls, and
continues so for a great distance, till passing a number of
tributary streams, it becomes perceptibly reduced in size, where
Mr. McKenzie was obliged to relinquish his enterprise on account of some sickness among his men: the current is unbroken
by rapids, and descends with great velocity; the country near
the falls resembles that on the main river, but from thence
upwards it is delightful beyond expression, the bottoms are
composed of an excellent soil, thinly covered with White
Oaks, Ash, Cottonwood, black Walnut, Birch, Hazel & Alder; the adjoining hills are gently undulating, with a sufficiency of Pines to give variety to the most beautiful Land-
scapes in nature.—The vallies are inhabited by innumerable
kinds of Elk, and the uplands are equally overstocked by
Deer and Bear.—few or no fish are found in its water, above,
and the Salmon & Sturgeon ascend no farther than the foot
of the Falls, this want is however well compensated for by
the incredible numbers of Beaver who inhabit its banks, which
from all accounts, exceeds any thing yet discovered on either
side of this continent.—The first nation above the falls are the
Cath-la-poo-qaas, supposed to be 300 strong; a little farther
up, on an Easterly branch live the Cath-lack-las of 80 men;
and along the river as far as Mr. McKenzie went, natives are
very numerous, and go by the name of shoo-shoo-nays, they
have neither horses nor Canoes; when they want to cross the
river, they prepare a large bundle of reeds, on which they
throw themselves and sweam a cross—their clothing is principally Beaver and Deer skins, they have no villages or sta-

tionary habitations, but live in temporary huts along the river banks—Mr. McKenzie says that their behaviour to him was respectful and obliging in the extreme.—

The general course of the river is about S.S. East[4]—we encamped for the night on a rising ground opposite the mouth; having come 23 miles against the exceeding rapid current.—

Saturday 4*th*—At the distance of 8 miles from last nights station is Vancouver's Point, as beautiful a piece of scenery as any the Columbia affords, it is composed of an enchanting meadow near the river bank, while the rear is a ridge of considerable elevation, moderately wooded with a variety of the Pine species; in the middle of the meadow stands a pond of pure limpid water, well stocked with Fish of different kinds, and in Spring and Autumn, the surface is covered with wild fowl,—23 miles higher, Quick sand river[5] enters on the south side—It is a rapid stream, about 80 yards wide, the length is unknown to the whites, but from Indian information it is of considerable extent, contains a good many Beaver, Elk and Deer,—In the main river opposite this is a ledge called the Seal Rocks (visible only in a moderate stage of the water) and frequented by members of these animals as a resting place.—a little lower down, a small creek comes in on the north side, is of no note, except its being the asylum of a few animals, whose skins are valuable; on an open spot, north side, and about 2 miles above quicksand, we pitched our Tents for the night,[6]—the total distance for to day was 33 miles.—

Sunday. 5*th*—Nothing worthy of remark occurred during this days march; we sailed the greater part, and at 4 P.M., having

[4] The Willamette River flows from this direction.
[5] Sandy River.
[6] About three miles south-southeast of Washougal, Washington.

come 23 miles, stopped on an island 5 miles below the rapids,[7] in order to prepare every thing for portage.—about 12 miles below this place, on the south side, is a very extensive Bluff with two small Cascades of at least 150 feet high; the face of the precipice is a smooth rock to where these falls project from the hill, but from thence to the top it is very curiously intersected by ravelins, which give it a strong resemblance to antique towers & fortifications.—[8]

The country through which we have passed to day is of a very unenviting aspect, rugged, barren, and mountainous, with the exception of a few small bottoms, the resort of a good many Elk & Bear.—

Monday 6th—We set out early with the hopes of being able to pass the rapids before night, but after proceeding about 2 miles, we had to encamp,[9] in consequences of strong appearances of bad weather.—

Tuesday 7th—Heavy rain fell during the greater part of yesterday afternoon; as soon as it ceased, every man's arms were put in the best order, and their cartridge Boxes replenished: this was a measure of precaution only, for altho' all the natives below assured us of the certain hostility of those who reside in this neighborhood, still our determination was to avoid everything like altercation, and to punish only where they were the wilful aggressors.—the party was accordingly divided in two brigades, the one to guard the heights immedi-

---

[7] Upper Cascades. They encamped on Hamilton Island.

[8] The group of falls including Multnomah and Bridal Veil.

[9] Lower Cascades. The island on which they spent the previous night was probably Hamilton, which lies at the lower end of the series of cascades. The present camp was probably on the north bank, about opposite the head of the island.

Astoria in 1811

From Tacoma Edition of Irving's Astoria
(New York, C. P. Putnam's Sons, 1897)

ately overlooking the River, to prevent surprise and protect those who were employed in dragging up the Canoes or carrying the goods along the margin of the rapids—but few indians came near us all day, and every thing went on although not fast, yet in the greatest safety and good order, till having ascended about 3 miles,[10] the large Canoe of Mr. D. Stuart, in passing between two large rocks, unfortunately touched the outer one, wheeled round, and before sufficient assistance could reach her, filled and upset, altho it was afforded with the greatest promptitude and alacrity; several of the packages floated off, but the greater part sunk not far below, the remainder were picked up by light canoes dispatched for the purpose.— On the supposition that some of the articles must have been caught by the residents of Strawberry Island,[11] I instantly embarked in a large Canoe, with 5 men and our interpreter, and had the good fortune to recover several small packages, with part of a Bale which had been taken up and was already divided among the *Captors;* I returned at sun set, and in crossing through a rapid, the water, which appeared as if it were boiling, gushed in at both sides of the canoe at such a rate as to creat real alarm for our safety—a few strokes of our paddles luckily extricated us from the danger, and we soon after reached the shore; had the canoe filled it would have upset in a moment, and no doubt can exist but every soul should have perished as we were a great way from the foot of the rapids,[12] the current like that of a mill sluice, and so rough that the ocean agitated by a tempest would be but a faint comparison.—

Wednesday 8th—The canoe which upset yesterday was very much damaged and unfit to proceed without being thoroughly

[10] To about the site of Bonneville Dam.
[11] Hamilton Island.
[12] That is, still above the foot of the rapids.

repaired; in the meantime I set out as before in the hope of getting the remainder of the bale of merchandise, as we were given to understand that it was at no great distance—after incessant paddeling in different directions for a long time, we discovered their receptacle, in a hut situated in a deep ravine nearly opposite our camp, and there recovered some of the package I expected, with the greater part of another; the Canoe was in sufficient order by night to hazard its being put again in the water, though still too crazy to risk any thing like a load in it.—This Canoe is the same with those made use of by the North West Company on this side of the rocky mountains, it is composed of Cedar boards ¼ of an inch thick, its only support within are a few braces or knees of the same material, ⅜ of an inch, to which the boards are secured with sturgeon twine, and the space which is caulked in Boats is here filled up with gum; Thus you have a vessel to answer the purpose of a bark Canoe, so far as regards facility of transportation, but in every other respect so much its inferior that no attempt at comparison can with justice be made; even in strength, the latter is far superior, for the bark will bend and give way to pressure (without material injury) which would split the Cedar one and send her to the bottom.—

Such canoes are very excellent in shallow water, long and bad portages, and may do tolerably in small and insignificant rapids, but nothing short of strong and well built Boats do I think fit to face the granit rocks of the grand rapids and Falls of the Columbia River: indeed I have no hesitation in saying that a Schenectady Boat, constructed of wood properly seasoned, would in the same situation of Mr. Stuart's Canoe have escaped with little or no damage.—remained in the same camp—

Thursday 9th—We renewed our daily toil at an early hour,

and after great labour and exertion, encamped late in the afternoon, about 1¼ mile further on.—[13]

Friday 10*th*—All hands were employed by the dawn of day, and we got along 1½ miles, without much interruption, untill a bluff point of rocks projecting far into the rapid obliged us to make a portage, upwards of 500 paces, to a small bay above, where we stopped for the night.—[14]

Saturday 11*th*   Those who were unnecessary in navigating the Boats went by land as a guard, and by breakfast time all were assembled at the low water portage—in coming up this morning, two of Mr. Clarks Canoes filled, but nothing was lost—from this place, the goods were carried half a mile, and the Boats got on by water, where the whole were again loaded and taken up the remaining rapids without diminishing their cargoes, except at two small points, where for greater safety part of the packages were landed. From last nights resting place to the head of the rapids is about 3 miles, & which we passed about 2 P.M., finding it rather early to halt, we continued on & encamped 2 miles above the grand Rapids.[15]

In low water by making a portage of two miles, you pass all the bad part of these cascades, and may *jump* the remainder without much risk, but in high water it is one continued rapid, from what is commonly the beginning of the portage to some distance below Strawberry island, which is nearly six miles—

The Indians at these rapids are composed of the Cath-lak-a-heckits & Cath-lath-la-las, each mustering about 150

[13] About the site of North Bonneville, Washington.
[14] At a point almost directly west of present-day Cascade Locks.
[15] About where the town of Stevenson, Washington, now stands.

warriors, are saucy impudent rascals, will steal when they can, and pillage whenever a weak party falls into their clutches.— Here is one of the first rate salmon fisheries on the River; they erect stages on scaffolds, to project some distance from the bank, by binding two long but slender trees together with strong withes, next tying a stout piece of wood across the two former, from 4 to 6 feet below where they are bound together.—thus arranged, this preparation is set erect in the water, when the ends of two slabs, several inches thick and from 20 to 40 feet long, are laid on the cross piece of the two uprights, so as to reach 6 to 8 feet beyond them, with the other ends resting on the rocks along the waters edge; at the farther extremity are a few of their boards from slab to slab, on which the Fisherman stands plying his scoop net; on the end of this erection, which stands on the shore, are placed huge stones, not only to be a counterpoise to the weight and exertions of the actor, but also to give it sufficient solidity to resist the impetuosity of the current—the places chosen are always a point where the water is strongest, and if possible a mass of rock a little outside the projection, between which the salmon are sure to pass, to avoid the greater body of the current —The net in use here is made fast in a large hoop, to which a very long handle is attached; the Fisherman pushes this to a depth of several feet perpendicularly in the water, allowing it to descend with the flood untill it encounters the Salmon, who, struggling to ascend, keep the net always distended, and is pulled up with such ease that boys are often employed, who succeed equally with the most robust man; the fish come this far by the middle of may, but the two following months are the prime of the season: during this time, the operator hardly ever dips his net without taking one and sometimes two Salmon, so that it is speaking within bounds when I say that an experienced hand would by assiduity catch at least five hundred daily—

Sunday 12*th*—The goods that got wet by Mr. Clark's canoe filling were this morning spread out to dry; and one of our young gentlemen sent back to the rapids for the Chiefs, with whom he returned about 11 A.M., when a council was held, after which they were presented with some tobacco &ct. and were told at the same time that it was given on account of their peacable & decorous behaviour, and that so long as they continued the same kind of conduct, they might always be sure of experiencing a reciprocal friendship with the whites—The goods were dry by the middle of the afternoon, when we proceeded 5 miles & encamped on the North side.—[16]

Here our Clatsop interpreter, meeting with two Indians from above, expressed a wish of returning to the rapids to procure the assistance of a friend, without whom he could not precisely interpret the language of the natives at the Falls.— his request was reluctantly granted, and he set off with a promise to rejoin us next day—

Monday 13*th*—We went on with a fine breeze all day, and stopped for the night 12 miles below the Falls[17]—passed two considerable creeks on the north, and one on the south side, in two of which, according to Indian information, Beaver is tolerably plenty—this tract of country is very barren and hilly, well wooded, and stocked with a good many Bear and Deer,—Came in all 25 miles.—

Tuesday 14*th*—This day at noon we arrived at the commencement of the long narrows,[18] discharged all our arms, cleaned, and reloaded them; here our Clatsop came up with us, accompanied by two Indians from below, which was very agree-

---

[16] About the site of Carson, Washington.
[17] The Dalles. They camped near the location of Lyle, Washington.
[18] Five Mile Rapids.

able to us all, as it was in passing these rapids we expected the savages would attack, were they in the least desirous of measuring their prowess with ours, in which case the having of an interpreter was of the first importance: we passed several inferior ripples, and encamped two hours before sun set, on the south side,[19] which is by far the best & shortest portage— here the whole company were divided into three equal parts to stand guard, 19 from dusk till 11 P.M.—19 from that untill 1 A.M. and the other 19 from one till day light; this precaution is to be continued untill we are above all the Falls and bad rapids—

Wednesday 15*th*—Matters went on but slowly, as the men had to make two trips with the canoes, on account of their number being reduced by a guard of 20 kept on the bank for the same purpose as at the lower rapids—a good many Indians kept about us all day, but were not suffered to come near the baggage or the men at work—at one place today the packages were carried 200 paces, and unremitted exertions only enabled us to get to this station, which is but 1½ mile from that of last night's—[20]

Thursday 16*th*—The goods were this morning transported by land 500 yards, to a large village where we breakfasted; they were again embarked for 250—when a portage of 880 paces succeeded, which brought us to the upper end of the Indian camp.—Here every thing was put in the canoes and towed along the rocks for one mile, to a fine sand beach, where we stopped for the night[21]—while in the vicinity of the Town,

[19] At a point five miles east of the site of The Dalles, Oregon.

[20] Up the bank from the previous camp, at about the head of Five Mile Rapids.

[21] About halfway between the site of The Dalles and the mouth of the Deschutes River.

the natives came about us in great numbers, but few were armed, and upon the whole they behaved much to our satisfaction; in consequence of which a present of Tobacco was given to the Chiefs—

Friday 17*th*—The first watch had scarcely taken their station last night when the Indians from below came running towards our camp: the word to arms was immediately given, and every man was at his post in an instant; the natives came up much out of breath, and nearly petrified with horror, related that a war party of Shosshonies had attacked one of their canoes late in the afternoon and killed 4 men and 2 women—our Clatsop was absent at this time, but he soon after arrived, and corroborated the statement we had just heard—not however putting too much confidence in the report, we hauled up the Boats and Canoes, of which and the packages a good breastwork was made on three sides, with the river in our rear,—the night passed without molestation, and we began with the dawn to make a portage of the remainder of the narrows;[22] as it was utterly impracticable to do any thing by water, the goods and vessels were first carried 200 yards from our camp, where a guard of ten men was posted as soon as the first parcel was laid down, and the other watch of ten remained untill all was taken away from our last night's station: in this way we passed the whole carrying place, never at any time being more than 300 paces between the resting places, by which means ten persons well armed were constantly on the look out at each end, while the others were perpetually going and coming, so that in case of an attack at least 20 men would be on the spot, and the whole could join in the course of two minutes.—

We reached the upper extremity by 4 P.M. and after making a present of Tobacco to the Chiefs of the two villages we

[22] Ten Mile Rapids.

passed to day, and the like to the sachem of a strong tribe on the north side, who rendered us the honor of a formal visit, went on about 1½ mile, where, on account of a heavy squall, we were obliged to encamp for the night.—[23]

Sunday 19th—Yesterday the wind continued too strong for us to move, and to day we had got no farther than within about half a mile of the Falls[24] when Mr. Clark's Boat became too leaky to proceed, consequently we were necessitated to encamp for the night in order to have her repaired.—

Monday 20th—We started with the dawn and got within 140 yards of the upper end of the Falls, without unloading, when by carrying the goods that distance, we got up our craft by water—The long narrows, Falls, and space between are inhabited by the Cheepan-chick-chicks 100, Cathlaskos 150, Ilth-kye-mamits 100, and Chilwits 200 strong; the three first have villages and live here constantly, but the last reside a little inland and come in the summer to fish; all mix promiscuously at this season, and the choice of stations is guided entirely by whim and caprice, or the attractions one fishing place has over another, besides most of the Indians near the Forks of the Columbia[25] assemble here to procure wherewith to pass the winter in greater comfort than the resources of their own country afford; so that when added to the residents of this quarter, 700 men might be collected in two hours.—The quantity of Salmon destroyed here, if put in figures, would exceed the bounds of credibility, so I must refer the imagina-

[23] At a point on the south bank almost directly opposite the location of Wishram, Washington.

[24] Celillo Falls.

[25] The meeting of the Snake and the Columbia rivers.

tion to its own conjectures for the number, which may be calculated in the ratio of what was mentioned at the grand Rapids as the produce of an expert scooper in one day: from this some idea may be formed on the immense shoals of Salmon which annually ascend the Columbia & its waters.—

Last spring in the prosecution of a voyage to Mr. David Stuart's establishment, with 2 Clerks and 14 Men, we got to the portage of the long Narrows early in the month of April; but being to few in number to transport the Canoes and Goods across the carrying place, I was necessitated to employ the Cathlascos for that purpose, and dispatched Mr. John Reed, with 5 men well armed, to guard the first load, but no sooner had they got fairly out of sight than their disposition to plunder became evident, and notwithstanding the men's utmost exertions, the villains carried off two bales of merchandise, with several small articles; and seeing that even this did not provoke the *long beards* to any hostile measure, they at length became so audacious as to pillage the poor fellows even of their knives and pocket handkerchiefs; word was soon brought me of these proceedings, and I made all possible expedition to join them (at the Indian village) but could not succeed untill dusk; it being impossible at such a late hour to better our forlorn situation till morning, the night was passed under arms, without one of us closing an eye, and when day was yet scarcely visible in the east, every thing was embarked, and we gladly bade adieu to the abominable den of miscreants—Elated I suppose by the success of yesterday, we were this day followed by the whole tribe, which by the time we reached the Falls was augmented in number to upwards of 400, armed principally with Bows and Arrows, but when these were defficient, war-clubs, Battle-axes &ct. were substituted.—Surrounded by this host, they requested permission to make the portage for us, which I declined by saying that it was now too late, but that if they behaved well, their offer might probably be accepted in the morning, and in the meantime engaged them to take up the Canoes, a service they executed with fidelity, but were no sooner accompensed for their trouble than they manifested an intention to distroy them; notwithstanding the presence of 8 Men, exceedingly well armed, whom I sent along as a guard, and were only at last prevented by the interference of an old man, who seemed to be a considerable personage among them—With the exception of about 50 the whole of this hostile band crossed to the north shore, soon after the termination of the hoary gentleman's lecture, which I suppose tended only to disuade them for the present, and to watch an opportunity to strike a more decisive blow: well aware that their proffered assistance was not for the best of purposes, I determined if possible to defeat their infernal machinations, and at 1 A.M. by the aid of moon light began the transport of the goods, with the hope of getting all over before the dawn —two loads only remained at day break, when those who had remained to watch our motions perceived what had been going on, and thinking themselves too weak for an attack, gave the alarm to those on the opposite side, who to about the number of 130 embarked in several large canoes—I immediately sent the people to the lower end for another load, with a request that Mr. Reed should keep what men he thought necessary with him, as I supposed the gentry from the other side were not crossing with any good intention, but he very imprudently refused retaining any of them, saying that Mr. McClellan & himself could protect what little remained—No sooner did the canoes touch the shore, than their *cargoes* leaped upon the rocks, and without the least hesitation made directly for the goods, beginning an indiscriminate pillage, which the two gentlemen vainly attempted to oppose—Hearing the war yell on their first arrival, I well knew my presence would be necessary, and with 8 brave fellows arrived to their assistance at this crucial moment, when we found Mr. Reed weltering in his blood, having received five Tomahawk wounds in the head.—Notwithstanding our sudden appearance with *presented arms,* not one of them seemed in the least alarmed, nor did they make any disposition to attack us, untill I called to the fellow who was mauling Mr. Reed to desist, or he should be shot instantly; this seemed to rouse them all, and some began to advance upon us in a very menacing manner; finding matters had gone this far, and that further forbearance would avail nothing, I formed the men, shewing a front two deep, and ordered the most advanced to shoot down the *brave* (who still continued beating Mr. Reed)   this was executed in a twinkling, when we gave a cheer, and charged, which so disconcerted our assailants as to produce an instant, and universal flight.—Mr. Reed (who by this time was lying senseless on the ground) we carried to the canoes, which were found too leaky to be put in the water, and the oars were still at the lower end of the portage; this unavoidable detention created much alarm among some of the men, particularly two young fellows, who became so terrified as *literally to faint away;* the moment they recovered their senses I ordered them to be deprived of their arms, their under clothes taken off, and a piece of cloth tied round the waist in imitation of a squaw, then stowed them away among the goods in one of the canoes; this ludicrous affair, in spite of the perilous situation we were placed in, excited considerable mirth and seemed to reassure a few, who were rather in a state of wavering between *fear* & *determination:*

The Indians having all crossed to the other side induced me to send some men for the oars, while the others were employed in caulking &ct. our water craft, which were shortly got ready, when we embarked and continued our voyage up the south side,—News of this affair no sooner reached the Cathlasco village than two horses were killed, and the blood, in its crude state, was drunk by the warriors in order to give them additional courage and intrepidity; this ceremony, with their dead dance and war song finished, they to the number of 450 men, clothed in their garments and furnished with every other accoutrement for war, mounted their horses and followed us panting for revenge; we however fortunately discovered them some distance above the Shooshonie river,[26] crossing to the side by which we were ascending, and when near the place, found them posted among cut rocks, close along which we must unavoidably pass—Finding they had the advantage of the ground, we stopped about 400 yards below, discharged and reloaded our arms, made a fire, and dressed Mr. Reed's head, in which were five gashes inflicted with a Tomahawk, of about two inches in length each; this done we fastened the canoes together, made fast to a rock at a small distance from the shore (from which we could retreat with facility in the event of being too hard pushed) and there awaited the onset—not long after, the war chief, with three of his principal warriors, came to us in a canoe, and after a long preamble told us that we had killed one and wounded another of his nation, that their relations, incensed, had compelled him to take command of the party, that they were come purposely to fight, determined to have satisfaction in some shape or other; proposed as the only means of appeasing their fury that we should deliver up Mr. Reed (who he observed was already on the verge of the grave) to the friends of the savage who fell, to be by them cut in pieces.—this would (he said) completely obliterate their present animosity, and that the greatest harmony would prevail for the future—Our answer was, *no*, the man wounded by the deceased is our brother, and you must destroy all of us before you get him; we are prepared and ready for your warriors, bring them on, and we will teach you a more serious lesson than you learned this morning: this they took some time to consider of, and after

[26] Deschutes River.

mature deliberation, the business was compromised, for a Blanket to cover the dead and some Tobacco to fill the Calumet of peace; they soon after recrossed to the north side and we saw no more of them.—

The country which at the Fort was an impenetrable wilderness, at the grand rapids began gradually to diminish in the quantity of timber.—small prairie knobs occasionally checquered the Landscape, and by the time we reached the foot of the long narrows, the woods were at a considerable distance behind us—From the sea to the rapids, the forests continue of nearly the same character, but a little farther up, the pines become stinted and intermixed with scrubby Oaks, which latter tree gains almost total ascendency as you approach the upper extremity of this wooded tract, apparently opposite *mount hood.*—

This mountain is entirely detached from any other, and when we consider the great height of the river hills (which in a civilized soil) would be thought impassable, from their magnitude, and above which this gigantic mass appears as a steeple overlooking the lower houses of a city, it will easily be imagined that it is not a hillock of the common order.—at present trees are discernable about half way up the acclivity, the tops of others in a higher region begin to emerge from the snow, but the summit never knows a change of seasons.—

Here the bluffs come close to the river, on both sides; along that of the north we pursued our course, crossed to the island opposite the Shooshonie river, and encamped some distance above;[27] this River has a considerable cascade near its entrance and is about 200 yards wide; nothing else is known of it, except its being inhabited by the Shooshonie nation, which signifies an inhabitant of the interior to distinguish them from those of the main River, who are called fish indians —about two days march up this stream, it is well wooded, &

[27] About two miles east of the mouth of the Deschutes River.

its banks are the asylum of a great many Bear, Deer, and Beaver,—

Tuesday 21st—At an early hour we continued our route along the south side, and at breakfast time recognized two of the villains who robbed Messrs. Crooks & Day last spring when on their way from St. Louis to Astoria; they being left behind by the rest of the party in consequence of their having suffered so much from privations and fatigues as to become too debilitated to keep pace with them—The two rogues were immediately seized, bound hand and foot, and thrown in one of the canoes; we then told the bystanders that so soon as the property pillaged was restored, they should be liberated: expresses were by them sent off in different directions, and before night they arrived with the two rifles, but the smaller articles could not be recovered: their bands were then loosened, and they departed with evident symptoms of terror, little expecting to get off with so much clemency—a small river[28] adds its tributary waves about 2 miles below where we encamped to night;[29] it is about 60 yards wide at its mouth, and issues from among high hills, entirely destitute of timber, as are also its banks, and the soil is nothing but sand—to day we were obliged to unload twice, in consequence of bad rapids, and came in all 18 miles.

Wednesday 22nd—We had a strong fair wind all day, which enabled us to sail 45 miles[30]—the country is without a stick of wood, and the soil is an entire desert of sand, even on the top of the bluffs.—

[28] John Day River.
[29] On the point formed by the bend made by the Columbia.
[30] To a point near the mouth of Pine Creek, which empties through the north bank of the Columbia.

Thursday 23*rd*—Light breezes of southy. wind prevailed the greater part of the day—the hills have now receded, and the columbian plains commence, with a similar quantity of land to that passed yesterday—the length of todays march is 30 Miles.—[31]

Friday 24*th*—We reached the Umatalla River before night, opposite which we encamped, having come 26 miles—This stream is 80 yards wide at its mouth, takes its rise in the mountains which bound the columbia plains to the south east; and is well stocked with Beaver.—

Saturday 25*th*—This day we found intolerably hot, and after coming 15 miles Stopped at an indian village,[32] where 4 horses were traded, having in the course of to days journey procured 5 others.—

Here we got some Lamper-eels, which with a kind of chub seem peculiar to these waters, above the Falls—remained here 26th—

Monday 26*th*[33]—We traded two more horses this morning, and continuing on 15 miles farther, passed the Wallawalla River (about 2 miles above which we met a number of indians, and encamped for the night[34]) this stream is 60 yards wide, takes its source with the Umatalla, and possesses a good many Beaver & Otter, and Deer in great numbers frequent its vicinity; near the entrance live the nation from whom it derives

[31] To a spot near the mouth of Glade Creek.

[32] About four miles up the bank from the site of Mottinger, Washington.

[33] The twenty-seventh rather than the twenty-sixth, as the text makes clear.

[34] About a mile below the site of Hover, Washington.

its name; they are good indians, about 200 strong, but as yet entirely ignorant of the mode, and destitute of the means, to ensnare the furred inhabitants of their lands—The natives of this neighborhood have but a scanty subsistence, when compared to those of the Falls, as their country possesses very few fishing places, and them being none of the best, they are consequently obliged to content themselves with a little venison and roots the greater part of the year: and they require great labour in hunting and extraction, so that a fellow who considers it a hardship to be industrious soon makes the best of his way to the Falls, where he can indulge his sloth without fear of starvation.—By such worthless dogs are these noted fishing places peopled, which like our great cities may with propriety be called the head quarters of vitiated principles.—

Tuesday 28*th*—Last night a great many indians accompanied by a few squaws of the Walla-wallas danced for a length of time, round a fire made for the purpose, at one end of our camp; this was to welcome us into their country, and their behavior evinced how much they were pleased at our passing the night among them.—From this band I procured 4 more horses, which completes the 15 necessary for our voyage, for all of which with their appendages, I gave merchandise to the amount of 179 $^{82}\!/_{100}$ Dollars, but had we been in possession of the proper articles, they should not have cost more than one half the value.—

In the afternoon we crossed the Columbia, encamped on the opposite side,[35] at the mouth of the Walla-walla, to which place we were escorted by Messrs. McKenzie Stuart & Clarke, with their people, except a detachment of those belonging to the latter, who repaired to the entrance of Lewis' River,[36]

[35] At the site of Wallula, Washington.
[36] The lower reaches of the Snake River were known by this name.

there to trade what horses were requisite to continue his inland expedition.—

Thursday 30*th*—Mr. Clarke left us this morg. with a strong westerly wind and although we made the best use of our time, both yesterday and today, yet it was evening before our pack-saddles and packages were perfectly prepared.—

Friday 31*st*—We had breakfasted, and were with our horses &ct. across the *creek*[37] by 7 A.M. when bidding (probably a last) adieu to our friends, we soon after entered the hills, and steered a S.S.E. course—the day was hot in the extreme, with just wind enough to raise the sand on the knobs sufficiently to produce an almost suffocating effect; we travelled without making any thing like a halt till sun set; over hills for the most part of moderate height, whose composition was of sand and brittle clay, in nearly equal proportions, without the least appearance of having experienced any share of the dew of heaven since the time of Noah Flood.—Towards dusk the ravines became less deep and the country gently undulating, but the shallow drains still bent their course to the Columbia. —already had a fine young dog (our only companion of the kind) given up for want of water; and Leclaire, to preserve respiration, drank his own urine, when despairing of finding a brook, we began to talk of stopping for the night.—Searching a little farther on for an eligible situation, we discovered by the faint remains of day light, at a great distance a head, something like a wood, in the vicinity of which we were confident of getting a supply of that element we so much wanted—a pace of the speedy kind took place of our common one, and at a late hour we reached the Umatalla, near a ripple

[37] Walla Walla.

which the Horses (I suppose) hearing, rushed forward to immediately and drank immoderately, then crossed to the other side, where a gravely beach being the first dry spot near, we took up our quarters on it for the night;[38] having come this day at least 45 Miles—

[38] About opposite the site of Pendleton, Oregon.

[August 1812]

Saturday August 1—In consequence of our long & laborious ride yesterday, the sun had gained considerable strength before any one seemed inclined to quit his rocky couch, and it was nearly 8 o'clock before we set out.

The river here is about 60 yards wide, full of small rapids, but too shallow to afford an asylum for any of the finny race: the bottoms are from 4 to 600 paces broad, well covered with cottonwood, possess a good many swamps & ponds, in which reside myriads of Beaver—

We continued up this stream 3 miles, when pursuing the same course as yesterday, over a level plain, we at the end of 20 more got on another fork, wooded in a similar manner, but except in holes totally destitute of water. encamped on the north side.—[1]

Sunday 2nd—Before sunrise our horses were loaded, and we proceeded 5 miles up the fork in an easterly direction, to where it divided into two branches; we took that from the south for 6 miles, to its final separation into small brooks, thence 6 more

---

[1] On McKay Creek, at a spot about eleven miles east by south from Pilot Rock, Oregon.

up the mountain, still going towards the mid day sun, then taking a dividing ridge, we went S.E. 8 more, and halted at 4 P.M. on a branch of the Glaize River.[2]—These mountains are the south east boundaries of the Columbia plains, and divide the *waters* of the *main river* from those of Lewis' in this quarter.—[3]

Monday 3rd—The sun appeared with unusual splendor in the east, just as we had regained our tract; the road was over very high hills, intersected by deep ravines for 4 miles due east, thence descending into the short drains of the branch where we lay last night.—We next made 9 S.S.E. to a considerable fork of the glaize,[4] then following that 3 more, between rocks and bluffs, encamped at 1 P.M., opposite a creek coming in from the south, which rather exceeds in magnitude the one we descended—[5]

Tuesday 4th—Not long after daylight we continued down the Creek till 9 A.M., when finding a deep hole with some salmon in it, we halted 4 hours, and speared seven.—Proceeded on again at 1 P.M., thro' a most enchanting tract (for a few miles) where the gloomy heavy timbered mountains subside into beautiful hills, chequered with delightful pasture grounds, which, when combined *with the* numerous rivelets murmuring over their gravely serpentine beds towards the glade below, afford a scene truly romantic, and such as is seldom to be met with in these regions of solitude and gloom.—We soon after

[2] Grande Ronde River. Actually he was on McCoy Creek rather than a branch of the Grande Ronde. They camped about seventeen miles west of La Grande, Oregon.

[3] The Blue Mountains, from which tributaries ran south and east to the Snake, north and west to the Columbia.

[4] McCoy Creek.

[5] About eighteen miles west-southwest of La Grande.

entered on a similar road to that of this morning, and stopped at sunset on the left bank—Two branches came in on each side of the creek, which is extremely crooked, although the general course is about N. East—

20 miles was the extent of this days march—[6]

Wednesday 5th—The sun had made its appearance above the cliffs when we left our last nights station, the road was rugged in the extreme, and the proximity of the mountains obliged us frequently to cross the river, a business our horses are by no means fond of: we went on but slowly, and at the end of 12 miles extricated ourselves from among rocks and precipices to enter the big flat, where on account of having broke several saddles, we encamped,[7] on the right bank one mile below the narrows, and in the evening shot two Salmon and a Beaver.—

Thursday 6th—The men were busily employed yesterday afternoon, and all today, making and mending saddles, which are at last completed and will enable us to set out early in the morning—

Friday 7th—It was 6 A.M. before our horses were collected and loaded; our route lay along the mountains, on the south side of the big Flat, for 11 miles; then winding to the east for 9 more, came to a gap, out of which issued a small branch, where we encamped for the night.[8]—about 7 miles from this place, to the westward and close to the hills, is a sulphur lake, 300 yards in circumference, fed by a spring in the south east corner, which appeared nearly 10 feet square and as greatly

[6] Eight miles due west of La Grande, on the left bank of the Grande Ronde River.

[7] On the site of La Grande.

[8] About two miles south-southwest of the site of Union, Oregon.

agitated as if boiling[9]—at a short distance, the vapour was excessively noisome, and for half a mile round the olfactory nerves were sensibly affected thereby—

It is much frequented by Elk, which animal is tolerably plenty in the adjacent mountains, and it would appear from their numerous horns, strewed every where round the pond, that they visit it mostly in the spring of the year; continuing a few miles farther through the plain, a large Creek comes from the S. E. and nearly opposite its mouth, another from the west, both of which join the Glaize River a little way above its re-entrance into the narrows, where it is upwards of one hundred yards wide. This plot is at least 60 miles in circumference, in but few places swampy, of an excellent soil, and almost a dead level; with the Glaize and its two branches just mentioned meandering in every direction through it—the banks of these streams are high and muddy, covered in particular places with dwarf Cottonwoods, and the residue in a large growth of Willows, which afford an inexhaustible stock of food for the incredible multitudes of the Furr'd race who reside in their bosoms, but the S. East fork excels both the others, particularly in the number of its inhabitants of the Otter tribe—A few Deer and Racoon are the only animals you may add to the Elk, Beaver, and otter as being natives of this tract—

The river at the extremity of this prairie is very deep, but it there enters a range of mountains,[10] much superior in size to those thro' which we descended along its borders—

It falls into the Snake or Kimooemee river, about 30 miles above its junction with the Pacheecum, and is called, by the aborigines at its entrance, Koos-koos-kee.—[11]

[9] Hot Lake, about seven miles northwest of Union.

[10] The Wallowa Mountains.

[11] This passage is confused. The Grande Ronde enters the Snake River about thirty miles above the Clearwater, sometimes known as the Kooskooskee. The Pacheecum may have been the Salmon River, which in turn enters the Snake about thirty miles above the Grande Ronde.

Saturday 8*th*—Set out late, and continued up the branch for 8 miles E.S.E. then 6 S.S.E. to the westerly bend of a large creek,[12] but whether it is the S.E. fork of the glaize, or a tributary stream of the Kenooemu,[13] am unable to say.—having gone 9 miles up this, through a high prairie, and crossed two considerable branches proceeding out of the mountains which bound this plain to the south,[14] encamped on the bank of the River,[15] some time before sun set.—

Sunday 9*th*—Our course today was about south, thro' the prairie and along the same stream as yesterday, 26 miles to where it issues from the mountains,[16] which are the highest in this quarter and run from E.S.E. to N.N.W.; at its entrance into this pile,[17] it is about 20 yards wide, the banks are very well supplied with willows and a good many Beaver, but the soil is very indifferent.—

Monday 10*th*—This days march was in all 27 miles, 14 miles of which were in a S.E. direction, up a small branch and over the dividing ridge, which is composed of low sandy hills, to a fork of wood-pile-creek,[18] then down that 13 E.S.E.[19]—When near the height of land, we saw no less than 19 antelopes, a sight so uncommon in this country that we in some measure, for a considerable time, doubted the evidence of our senses— We tried all possible means to get a shot at some of them, but they were so exceedingly shy as to avoid our (every en-

[12] Powder River.
[13] Snake River.
[14] A spur of the Blue Mountains extending eastward to the Snake River.
[15] About two miles north of the site of Haines, Oregon.
[16] To the site of Baker, Oregon.
[17] The river's exit from the mountains.
[18] Burnt River. The "fork" was Alder Creek.
[19] On Alder Creek, to a point six miles east-southeast of the location of Pleasant Valley, Oregon.

deavour at a near) approach—This animal is already to well described by naturalists for me to attempt any addition on that head.—

Tuesday 11*th*—Continued down the Branch for 4 miles, which leaving were in 4 more on the main body of the Creek,[20] which we followed for about 8, where the bottoms become large and of a sandy soil, in some places mixed with large brown gravel, with a great many Cotton wood and willow.—3 miles through the hills was the next part of our tract, to a small [northerly] rivelet, 3½ along that to the river again, and 4½ to the bend, where we crossed, and encamped,[21] having come in all 27 miles S.E.—

Wednesday 12*th*—in the first part of this morg. march, the hills came very close to the creek on both sides, which made the road very stoney and bad—The stream is still about 30 yards wide, abundantly furnished with willow and contains many Beaver—having followed it 17 miles S.E., came to an indian fishing place, where the Creek making a short turn to the north,[22] we quitted it, and in 7 miles reached the Snake river, proceeding up which 3 more brought us to our station for the night—[23]

This river is here about 400 yards in breadth, has high sandy banks, little or no willow, and a rapid current.—it is the main branch of the right hand fork of Lewis' river, called by Lewis and Clarke, Wimoo-enem. by some Indians, Ku-eye-nem, by the Snakes, Byo-paa,—and by the generality of

[20] Burnt River.

[21] At a spot about eight miles north-northwest of the site of Lime, Oregon.

[22] At the location of Huntington, Oregon.

[23] On a point about seven miles west-northwest of the present town of Weiser, Idaho.

whites, the Snake River:[24] immediately below this, it enters
the mountains, which become gradually higher to the end of
150 miles, where the whole body of the river does not exceed
40 yards in width, and is confined between precipices of astonishing heighth: cascades and rapids succeed each other, almost
without intermission, and it will give a tolerable idea of its
appearance were you to suppose the river to have once flowed
subterraneously through these mountains, and that in process
of time, immense bodies of rock were occasionally detached
from the ceiling, till at length the surface of the heights descended into the gulph and forms at present the bed of this
tumultuous water course—Mountain, here, appears as piled
on mountain, and after ascending incessantly for half a day,
you seem as if no nearer the object in view than at the outset—

From the accounts of Messrs. McKenzie & McClellan,
this kind of country continues for about 300 miles, by the meanders of the river, which is very crooked: their tract last fall
was as near the bank as possible, but were often compelled
to leave it by the intervention of impervious masses of rocks.—
they were in all 12 persons, took 21 days constant travelling
to the Mulpat river,[25] and subsisted during that time on an
allowance by no means proportionate to the bodily labour they
daily underwent.—being no more than two Ibex[26] and 5
Beaver, the skins of which they preserved, and subsisted on
for the last 5 days; the best, and indeed only method of dressing those skins, is, first to singe them well, after which they
must be boiled for several hours, then cut into small pieces,
so as to be fit for bolting or gulping, which is a well known
practice among the *York Shire Men* in feeding on fat pork—

Messrs. Hunt and Crooks, with 39 men, subsequently at-

[24] Stuart apparently conceived of the Snake and the Clearwater as flowing
together to form the Lewis River, though by this reckoning the Snake should
have been the left fork.

[25] The Little Salmon River, or one of the adjacent waterways.

[26] Here probably antelope, rather than mountain sheep.

tempted a passage thro' these narrows, in December, but the snow was too deep, and the country being entirely destitute of game, they were compelled to relinquish their undertaking, after the former had penetrated 120 miles, and the latter (with 18 men) 30 farther—They returned and ascending wood pile creek, went to the Umatalla by the route we have now come, where they found the Scyatogas,[27] and got relief—This nation is about 250 strong, and possess that tract of country bounded on the South east by the Bigflat, on the North by Lewis' river, on the West by the Columbia, and on the South by the Walamat, comprising an extent of nearly 100 miles square, intersected by many handsome streams, which are all well stocked with those animals we have come so far in quest of.—but untill now, the natives having had little inducement to diminish their numbers, they remain'd in undisturbed possession of their native soil.—

This tribe as well as the Flatheads (who are reputed to be excellent Indians, about 1,800 warriors, and inhabit that tract of country situate between Lewis' River and the north west branch, or main Columbia, bounded in the rear by the Rocky Mountains) own immense numbers of horses, a great proportion of which run wild in these boundless plains, and are often the red and white man's only dependence for *food*— These two nations are less theivish, and much more cleanly, than any of their neighbors; but they are of a haughty and imperious disposition, very impatient of insult and revengeful in the extreme; however by proper treatment, they might be rendered the best and most useful division on this side of the mountains.—

Thursday 13*th*—We continued up the south side of the River for 19 miles, in an E.S.E. direction, and encamped[28]—an Indian came to our camp late in the evening with the grateful

---

[27] Nez Percé.   [28] Opposite the site of Weiser.

tidings of two white men living with his people, about a days march above—

Friday 14th—The river makes a turn at almost right angles —we went in 20 miles to a creek 50 yards wide, with numerous Willow and Beaver along its banks, crossed it, and at the end of 6 more S.S.E. stopped for the night[29]—during this days march the bottoms were very extensive, covered principally with salt wood, except near the river, where there are some willows, but they overflow so much in the spring season as to render them a perfect swamp.

The hills are low, of a sandy soil, and like the high bottoms, the same shrub predominates.—

Saturday 15th—Proceeding on due south, we struck the bends of the river from time to time, till having come 25 miles, we found a creek 70 yards wide, in every thing resembling the one passed yesterday, where we found ten lodges of Shoshonies, or Snakes—These people giving us to understand that some whites were on the other side of the river, we encamped in the neighborhood of their huts,[30] and dispatched an Indian in quest of the men we had heard of, supposing them to be either those left by Mr. Crooks in the Winter, or the Hunters who remained in the rocky mountains last fall—[31]

Opposite our present station, a large River[32] comes in from the east, is well timbered, contains many Beaver, and is the most renowned fishing place in this country; it is consequently the resort of the majority of the Snakes, where incredible numbers of Salmon are taken, forming, with esculent

[29] About two miles south of the site of Ontario.
[30] On the Owyhee River.
[31] These men were members of exploring parties sent out from Astoria the previous year.
[32] Boise River.

roots, the principal article of food which the natives of this barren tract possess—28 miles below is another large creek, and 16 still lower down is wisers River, a stream 60 yards wide, well stocked with small wood and Beaver, in which the former strikingly resembles it—

Last night the musquitoes assailed us in innumerable host, and completely deprived our eyelids of their usual functions; even after the dew had fallen, these infernal pests still continued their music to our no small annoyance.—

Sunday 16th—Finding our information incorrect regarding the people, we crossed the Creek early in the morning, and sometime after were overtaken by the Indian who guided the party over mad river mountain[33] last fall; he said that he parted ten nights ago with 3 of our hunters, who had caught a great many Beaver, but that the Absarokas (Crow Indians) had discovered the place where their hunt was concealed, and carried off every thing.—That the others had lost their horses and were stripped by the same nation, with whom they at present were—the 3 whom he lately saw were on their way down, had only a horse each, and but one Rifle among them; their names he said are, Alexis, Michel, and Mackaw—hearing that there is a shorter trace to the south than that by which Mr. Hunt had traversed the Rocky mountains,[34] and learning that this Indian was perfectly acquainted with the route, I without loss of time offered him a Pistol, a Blanket of blue

[33] Teton Pass, on the present Idaho-Wyoming line.

[34] The route referred to by the Indian was to become a section of the Oregon Trail. About one hundred miles south of Teton Pass, it crossed the present Wyoming line at the Bear River to enter the Green River plain at a point almost opposite South Pass, where the covered wagons were to cross the Continental Divide. Though the exact course was not known to him, Stuart decided to attempt the suggested route rather than Hunt's trail over Teton Pass. It was this decision that led him on September 7 to turn south along the Portneuf River rather than continue along the Snake.

Cloth, an axe, a knife, an awl, a fathom of blue Beads, a look-
ing-glass, and a little Powder & Ball, if he would guide us
from this to the other side, which he immediately accepted,
saying that salmon were not so good as La Vache (which signifies Buffalo), and returned to the wooded River,[35] for his
Arms &ct., promising to rejoin us tomorrow morning—we
went 10 miles south, and 19 more, turning gradually to the
N.East, where we encamped—[36]

Monday 17*th*—The Flies are [or] musquitoes tormented our
horses greatly over night, causing them to ramble to a considerable distance, which made it late before they were collected and loaded—about 4 miles from Camp, we met our
guide, who had crossed the River yesterday evening and slept
some distance above, went 5 more, where the Indian said the
nearest road was across the hills, but as it would take nearly
a day to reach the River again, advised our encamping;[37] having come no more than 9 miles, in about an E. course.—

Tuesday 18*th*.—We arose with the dawn, but our guide was
missing, and on collecting our horses, found the Indian's and
mine were gone—From his former good conduct, we had not
the least suspicion that he would attempt committing an act
of this nature, but following the tracks for some distance, were
convinced of his being the perpetrator, as they made towards
the water a few miles above our camp and crossed to the opposite side; we went 26 miles S.E. over the same kind of ground
we have passed for the last four days—[38]

[35] Boise River.
[36] Near the mouth of Sucker Creek.
[37] At about the site of Marsing, Idaho.
[38] At a point seven miles west of the location of Melba, Idaho.

Wednesday 19*th*—The excessive heat that has prevailed since we left wood pile Creek is very much diminished, and the suffocating, sultry nights have given place to agreeably cool ones, in consequence of which our musquitoe serenades are so irregular that it is only now and then we hear the song of a solitary warbler—The cause of this decrease in our nocturnal tormentors is owing to the nearly total disappearance of the river bottoms, for the hills are now in the neighborhood, and the declivities serve as its banks—our relief from torments has not been of long duration, for another nearly allied in blood to the former assail us most unmercifully, in innumerable *hordes,* for the greater part of the day—so that the sand Flies, these champions of light, may verily be paired with the imps of darkness—

Our route to day was mostly along the margin of the stream, 12 miles S. East, to the first perpendicular Bluffs on this side—these coming too near the waters edge, to afford a passage for our horses, we went up a drain 6 miles due south; then ascending the hills and steering S. East over a level plain, in 18 more struck a bend of the river where we took up our lodgings.—[39]

Concluding from our lesson of yesterday morg. that no dependence could be placed on the Indians, notwithstanding their uniform good behaviour and the praises lavished on them for rectitude and integrity of conduct by all the whites who have travelled through this country, we determined to keep a constant guard during the remainder of this voyage, the night to be divided into three watches and one person to stand at a time.—In the vicinity of our camp is a lodge of Shoshonies, so miserably poor that they could not furnish us even with a fish—

[39] About four miles below the mouth of Castle Creek.

Thursday 20—Went east by South 12 miles, across two bends, where, approaching the river to drink, we found John Hoback, fishing, and in an instant, Mr. Miller, Edward Robinson, and Jacob Reznor, who had been similarly employed, came out of the willows and joined us—They had, on leaving the party at Henry's Fort[40] last fall, gone 200 miles south, where they made that seasons hunt on a River which must discharge itself into the Ocean to the Southward of the Columbia;[41] from thence they steered 200 more due east,[42] where they found about 60 lodges of Arapayhas, who are an out law'd band of the Arapahoes; they robbed them of several horses, as well as the greater part of their clothing &ct.; they then left them, and continued their journey 50 miles, where they wintered, and early in the spring were overtaken by the same Rascals, who then robbed them of the remainder of their horses, and almost every thing else;—with half of the ammunition left, they purchased back two of their own horses, and after travelling about 950 miles, in which they suffered greatly by hunger, thirst, and fatigue, met us almost in a state of nature, without even a single animal to carry their baggage; Cass, one of their party, having villanously left them with one of the horses while on the head waters of the *big horn;*[43] and the other was stolen by the snake Indians, on this side of the Rocky mountains—For the greater part of their route, scarcely quadrupid or Bird came within reach of their guns, and the Inhabitants of the waters were their only means of subsistence during this arduous and tedious journey—

[40] A group of cabins built by Andrew Henry and others of the Missouri Fur Company's party on Henry's Fork at about the location of the town of St. Anthony, Idaho. The party wintered here in 1810, abandoning the post the following spring.

[41] Probably the southerly reach of the Bear River, which empties into the Great Salt Lake.

[42] Into south central Wyoming.

[43] Probably a confluent of the Green River, rather than the present Big Horn.

They say that all the southern water courses visited by them are abundantly stocked with Beaver, of the largest size and best quality they ever beheld, particularly in the vicinage of the mountains—All the unknown Indians they became acquainted with during their perambulation in that quarter are a southern band of Snakes, the Arapahays, who may probably muster 350 warriors—the Arapahoes 2,700, and the Black arms,[44] about 3,000 strong; the two latter nations are generally at enmity with each other, but are very friendly to the whites, and possess the best beaver country on this side of the mountains—particularly the latter, whose territories extend to the neighborhood of the Spaniards—

After regaling our half famished friends with the best our small pittance of luxuries could afford, we proceeded along the banks of the river for 3 miles, to a good fishing and grazing place, where we took up our lodging, for the night.—[45]

Friday 21*st*—We this day cut off the turns of the river, as usual, and at the end of 16 miles east, found 30 lodges of Snakes, encamped on the banks of Rocky bluff creek,[46] who, having some horses, we took up our quarters at a small distance below, hoping to get a few, as we are much in want of these animals since the late augmentation of our number, they having all determined on accompanying us to St. Louis.

They brought and traded a good many salmon, for Awls &ct.—but appeared by no means fond of parting with any of their horses—This creek is 20 yards wide, issues from among hills, which give its name, & the banks are without a twig; it runs from S.S.E. to N. of West,—

The few Salmon it contains are far better than we had reason to expect from the shallowness of its water—

---

[44] Utes.   [45] About a mile below the site of Grand View, Idaho.
[46] Bruneau River.

A Crow Lodge

From Catlin's North American Indians

Saturday 22*nd*—Strong were the inducements we held out for a few horses, but they withstood all our temptations, saying they had not a sufficiency for themselves, consequently we were obliged to content ourselves by exchanging two worn out ones for a couple that were vigorous and fresh—We crossed the creek at a late hour, and ascending the Bluff, our road was due east, over a barren plain, for 12 miles—where again striking the river, we went 4 miles S.E., mostly along its banks, to the next narrows; then leaving them to our left, in 6 more east, reached a bend of the main stream, where we encamped.—[47]

Sunday 23*rd*—Our route lay along the river bank all day, partly on the sides of the hills, which are close to the stream and very stony, but mostly through salt-wood barrens and low sandy plains—

Scarce and bad indeed is the fodder of our horses—what little we can procure being generally the rankest grass, and coarse weeds—a few Shoshone or Snake Camps were passed today, who have to struggle hard for a livelihood, even though it is the prime of the fishing season in this country—so poor are they that we seldom or never can get even a single salmon of them—Our whole march today was 21 miles E.S.E.—[48]

Monday 24*th*—The sun was an hour high before we had taken up our line of march, continued as near the river as the bluffs would admit—cut across a large bend over a hilly road, and at the end of 12 miles East—struck the stream again, which has much decreased in width and is full of rapids—

From hence turning gradually to the S. East, the road was very rough and stony for 18 miles more, where, finding

[47] Nine miles west of the site of Hammett, Idaho.
[48] To about three miles southwest of the site of Glenns Ferry, Idaho.

a small patch of grass and the country looking fully worse a head, we thought it most prudent to stop for the night,[49] in order to let our jaded steeds bring up their leeway—saw some Indians on the opposite side, swimming after dead and wounded salmon, which were floating on the surface of the water—

Tuesday 25th—We went 2 miles east, 1 S. East, to Cascade Creek,[50] which comes in on the North side and is 20 yards wide at the mouth, but altho' the banks are literally lined with Willow, other appearances preclude the idea of its being the asylum of any great number of the furred race; one mile more same course brought us to the Salmon falls, where we found about 100 lodges of Snakes, busily occupied in killing and drying fish—

The perpendicular pitch is on the north side, and upwards of 20 feet, but towards the south, it might more properly be called a series of cascades—

The fish begin to jump soon after sunrise, when the Indians in great numbers, with their spears, swim in to near the center of the Falls, where some placing themselves on rocks, and other to their middle in water, darts on all sides, assail the salmon, who, struggling to ascend and perhaps exhausted with repeated efforts, become an easy prey—with the greatest facility, prodigious numbers are slaughtered daily; it must have been from this place that the dead and wounded came, which we saw picked up by the starving wretches below; it is the most inconceivable thing in the world to me why those poor creatures do not prefer mingling with their own nation at this immense fishing place (where a few hours exertion would produce more than a months labour in their own way) rather than depend on the uncertainty of a fish ascending

[49] Four miles south of the location of Bliss, Idaho.
[50] Big Wood River.

close along shore, or catching a part of the few wounded that make their escape from these falls—

Their spears are a small straight piece of Elks horn, out of which the pith is dug, deep enough to receive the end of a very long willow pole, and on the point an artificial beard is made fast by a preparation of Twine and gum.—This point of horn is about seven inches long, and from a little below where the pole enters, a strong string of the same length is attached, which is fastened in like manner to the handle, so that when the spearsman makes a sure blow, the wicker catches, pulls off the point, and leaves the salmon struggling, with the string through its body, while the spear is on one side and the handle on the other,—the string is an excellent and necessary invention, for were they to depend on the spear without it, so slender is their construction that it would require at least six to make and mend these instruments in sufficient numbers for the use of one spearer—

Mr. Miller says that they stopped here on their way down,[51] it was in the afternoon, by far the best spearing time, when to his utter astonishment the Indians in a few hours killed some thousands of fish; and one salmon (in particular) leaped, in the presence of himself and others, from the commencement of the foam at the foot of the pitch clear over all the water-falls, which in my opinion must have been upward of 30 feet—Having soon traded what we wanted, our road was up the river 3 miles south—1 due west up the hills—5 S. West on the highlands, 4 east to the water, at some considerable rapids—then 5 miles S.E. across the uplands, to the mouth of muddy Creek,[52] where we stopped for the night—

Wednesday 26th—Muddy creek is 20 yards wide, the banks tolerably covered with willow, and comes from among barren

[51] Miller had made a previous trip into this area, going as far east as the present Wyoming line.

[52] Salmon Falls Creek.

hills in the south west,—Crossed it easily, & went 5 miles S.E. to the main stream, then along that 13 more east, to where the iron bound bluffs put in very near on both sides, at this place the path ascending the aclivity, and not knowing when we could reach water, we thought it most advisable (tho' early) to encamp[53]—Two Indians, their squaws, and one child came from below with five horses; they said their road was the same as ours and wished to travel in company, in expectation of which they tarried with us all night.—

Thursday 27*th*—This morning Jones caught a Beaver, and I traded a horse from the Indians—

As the property hid by Mr. Hunt last fall, when he abandoned the Canoes, is only about 50 miles from our present station, and knowing all would go did these fellows discover the place, I thought it best to remain here to day, which will be of infinite advantage to our horses, as they are much in want of rest and the grass is very good; by this days march, the savages will be too far off for us to fear being seen by them while taking out &ct. of the Cache, what articles belong to the gentlemen & Canadians along with me—

Friday 28*th*—We ascended the bluffs early, and following the trace in 9 miles S.E. crossed precipice creek,[54] up which we continued 14 more, and encamped[55]—The banks of this stream, at and some distance above its discharge, are almost 300 feet perpendicular, but as you progress upward, they gradually diminish in height and recede from each other, till small willow bottoms of from 20 to 50 yards wide occasionally vary the eternal rocky sameness of the river sides—

[53] About six miles north-northwest of the site of Filer, Idaho.
[54] Rock Creek.
[55] About two miles southwest of the site of Kimberly, Idaho.

Saturday 29*th*—The Indian path going by far too much to the south for our purpose, we, on leaving Camp, steered E. by S. for 30 miles, over what is (in this Country) called a prairie, but Forest of worm wood is more properly its name—we again struck the main river, at the Caldron Linn,[56] where one of the unfortunate Canoes[57] was lodged among the rocks, but although we wished on several accounts to see in what state she was, the Bluffs intimated that to gratify our wish we must risk our necks, so we of course declined it—Continuing on same course for 12 more, occasionally in sight of the water, and where it was hidden from the eye, the ear could with facility conduct us thither—

Being now in the neighborhood of the Caches and finding good grass, we unloaded and took up our quarters[58]— Anxious to know what state the property was in, I proceeded in company with Messrs. Crooks & McClellan to the spot, where to our astonishment we found six of them open, and except a few *Books,* which lay scattered in every direction by the wind, the whole of the contents had vanished—From appearances they had been taken up some time in the summer, and the Wolves were undoubtedly the beginners; these, attracted no doubt by the skins they contained, had paths beaten every where round, which there is reason to believe was what directed the Indians to the place.—

We had some thunder and a heavy gust of rain this afternoon, which is the first storm worthy of notice we have experienced since leaving the Wallawalla,—of all the Canoes left here by the party last fall, three only remain, and these too much shattered to be fit for actual service—

[56] "Linn" is a Scottish word denoting the pool at the bottom of a waterfall. Caldron Linn is situated at the entrance of Dry Creek.

[57] The wrecked canoe was a relic of Hunt's trip overland from St. Louis to Astoria. He had passed along the Snake River the previous year.

[58] About seven miles east-northeast from the site of Murtaugh, Idaho. The caches, like the canoes, had been left by Hunt.

Thirty miles below our present station is a fall of 50 to 60 feet,[59] from whence to this spot the river banks, on both sides, are nothing but cut bluffs of rock, at least 300 feet perpendicular and giving strong indications of Iron; there is in some places a beach under the Cliffs, but seldom of any extent and principally composed of immense masses of rocks, which have from time to time been hurled from the adjacent precipices—But for the greater part, nothing that walks the earth could possibly pass between them and the water, which in such places is never more than 60 feet wide, rushing with irresistable impetuosity over a bed of such rocks as makes the spray fly, somewhat similar to the surf of the ocean breaking violently on a lee shore; in particular spots, the stream expands to the breadth of 50 yards, but its general breadth for the 30 miles in question is from 30 to 35 yards, and in one place (at the Caldron Linn) the whole body of the river is confined between two ledges of rock somewhat less than 30 feet apart, and here indeed its terrific appearance beggars all description—Hecates Caldron was never half so agitated, when vomiting even the most diabolical spell, as is this vortex in a low stage of the water, and its bearing in idea such a proximity of resemblance to that, or something more infernal, I think well authorizes it to retain its new name, more particularly as the *tout ensemble* of these 30 miles has been baptized *"The Devils scuttle hole"*

One mile above is Clappins Rapid, so named from a poor fellow of that name being there drowned last fall in the parties' descent, when Mr. Crooks' Canoe split, filled, and upset.

Here, as I have already partially observed, the party were obliged (from the badness of the navigation) to abandon their Canoes and travel on foot to the Falls of columbia, a distance of 790 miles; from thence, they proceeded to As-

[59] Probably Auger Falls.

toria by water, having with much difficulty procured conveyance from the Natives—

Sunday 30*th*—Having nothing to eat, I dispatched Jones and Reznor up the river, to try what either their guns or Traps could produce, and proceeded to open the remaining 3 Caches, where we found a few dry goods, Traps, and ammunition, out of which I furnished Robinson, Reznor, and Hobach, as far as lay in my power, with everything necessary for a two year's hunt, which they are to make on this river below Henry's Fork, prefering that to returning in their present ragged condition to civilized society—Mr. Millers curiosity and desire of travelling thro' the Indian countries being fully satisfied, he has determined on accompanying us—

Messrs. Crooks & McClellan fished the greater part of to day and caught 13 Trout, which with a little Rice made our frugal and not over plenteous supper—The Chub have entirely disappeared, and a very excellent species of Trout supplies their place, a change we are by no means sorry for, as the former are by far the most worthless of the finny race.

Monday 31*st*—Several Traps were set last night, but furnished nothing for that very desirable operation, *the wagging of the jaws,*—every person was busily employed all day, mending saddles &ct., and in the evening we closed the Caches, having taken out what belonged to the people, with a few small articles necessary for this expedition; and put in a part of what merchandise I brought from Astoria, being convinced they were only a superfluity which served to encrease our baggage—The Books and Papers were carefilly collected, put into one of the old receptables, and covered snugly up—

[September 1812]

Tuesday September 1st—Having written two letters for Mr.
Reed, I stuck one on a pole near the place of deposit and gave
the other to Robinson, in order to ensure, if possible, some
mark of our being here in safety, as also of the destruction of
the property—about 20 days after we parted at the Walla
walla river, he was to set out from Lewis' fork for the express
purpose of finding those Hunters and to carry down whatever
was put in the ground at this place last Fall—If no accident
happens, he must be here ere long, and as these men are still
in great want of many necessaries, they will wait his arrival,
which is the more desirable as the only Canoe fit for a person
to risk himself in is on this side, and it would be impossible
to succeed in rafting the river, it being so full of rapids—At
a late hour we left our camp, and carried the hunters things
about 6 miles up the river, where they say Beaver enough can
be procured to support them, sometime—about 6 farther on,
we found Jones & Reznor, having caught two Beaver only,
one of which we took, and leaving the latter to return to his
companions, the former mounted his horse, and we (once
more seven in number) continued on for 3 Miles, and crossing
a small creek, encamped on its banks[1]—Our course to day was
east 15 miles—

[1] At the site of Burley, Idaho.

Saw a number of Antelope, which were so exceedingly wild as not to allow our approach within a mile—

Wednesday 2nd—We renewed our march at an early hour, the bluffs and hills have at length receded to a great distance on the north; and those on the side are also some miles from the river—the banks are thickly clothed with Willows and mostly low, the highest not exceeding 30 feet, and along both, great numbers of Beaver have their houses—

The whole face of the country appears level before us, a sight we have scarcely been indulged with, even in miniature, since we left the Columbia Plains, than which these seem far more extensive, and like them, the sage, Worm wood, & salt wood cover a parched soil, of sand, dust and gravel—

Leaving the river a few miles from last nights camp, we followed a small trace in about an E.S.E. direction to the hills, which we found tolerably well clothed with cedars & pines, the Indian lodge trace passing along the foot, we kept it till, supposing ourselves 20 miles farther on our journey, we stopped for the night, on a small brook of excellent water—[2]

Thursday 3rd—Last night, and untill 10 A.M., the weather was disagreeably cool—we set out early, and pursuing the Indian route for 23 miles E.S.E. struck a creek 30 feet wide,[3] with many Willows and some Beaver—Here we found 5 lodges of Shoshonies, from whom we procured a Dog, a little dried Salmon, and an excellent sort of Cake made of pulverized roots, and service Berries, with the unpleasant information of our having left the right tract some distance back, to regain which we must go down the creek; taking their advice,

[2] Two miles west of the site of Declo, Idaho.
[3] Marsh Creek.

we continued along the right bank for 5 miles, in nearly a north direction, and encamped;[4] having come in all 28 miles.—

Friday 4th.—Last night we made a hearty meal on the Dog's carcase, and between the evening's and this mornings pastime caught a sufficiency of Trout for breakfast, which we found delicious, they being fried with the dogs fat and a little Flour we had still preserved—

Leaving the creek to the left, we soon found and followed the lodge trace for 14 miles E.S.E. to Trout Run;[5] here we unloaded the horses and plied our fishing rods for two hours with indifferent success—then resumed our journey, and after sunset stopped on a low point, on the bank of the main stream[6]—which we kept in sights all this afternoon, and is from Trout run about 16 miles N.N.E.—

Saturday 5th—Caught a small Beaver last night, and at a late hour continued our journey over a pretty level tract, along a very rapid part of the river for 12 miles N. by E., when reaching portage Falls,[7] we again tried our lines and drew out a few Trout—These falls are about 35 feet high on the west side, but are little else than a series of Cascades on the east—The whole body of the stream is here scarcely 60 feet wide, but immediately above expands to the breadth of half a mile, with little or no current and the banks sufficiently covered with Willows to afford a plentiful supply of food for the incredible numbers of furred animals who inhabit its borders—

The country passed since yesterday morning has improved greatly—the sage, and its detestable relations, grad-

[4] Six miles east by south from the site of Declo.
[5] Raft River.
[6] On the Snake River, at the mouth of Rock Creek.
[7] American Falls.

ually decrease, and the soil though parched produces provender in abundance for our *Cattle*.—At the end of 3 miles due north, above the Falls, we took up our nights quarters, close to the river—[8]

Sunday 6th—Today our course was E.N.E. 23 miles, on the top of a tolerably level ridge, with a channel of the river[9] meandering along its base; the main body is a great way off and appears thickly clothed with willows, over which we often discover the foliage of trees, supposed to be cotton wood, and as far as the eye can reach, heavy timbered bottoms seem of such magnitude as to hide every vestige of undergrowth—two families of shoshonies came and encamped[10] close by us this evening, from whom we got some dried salmon and a Horse, for which I was obliged to give an enormous price—

Monday 7th—The Indian, notwithstanding the extravagant price I gave for his horse, regretted his bargain, brought back the goods, and begged permission to retain him; this I was not much inclined to assent to, but considering the great distance we had to travel through their country and the facility of stealing those animals, I thought it best to save at least the articles given him rather than run the risk—

2 miles E.N.E. brought us to the falls creek,[11] so called from its numerous cascades; it is from 40 to 50 yards wide, has good banks, some willow, and Beaver—This being the water course that guided Mr. Miller to the snake river, and

[8] At a spot now covered by the lake formed by the dam at American Falls.

[9] Actually the Portneuf River, rather than a channel of the Snake.

[10] To a point seven miles northwest of the site of Pocatello, Idaho. This place, like the previous campground, now lies beneath the lake.

[11] At this point Stuart arrived at the junction of the Portneuf and Ross Fork. Perhaps mistaking the fork for the main branch, he referred to the Portneuf as Falls Creek.

having determined (by very urgent persuasions) to take his tract, as less circuitous and more out of the *walks* of the Blackfoot Indians, who are very numerous and inimical to the whites, than that by Henry's Fort, we, soon after leaving camp, parted with the Indians and followed up the left bank for 25 miles S.E. then encamped a mile above the discharge of a small branch, coming in from the west—[12]

Tuesday 8th—We went 10 miles E.S.E. to the Forks when learning that the main, or most easterly, one was very rocky and a bad road, we took the other,[13] and followed it 5 miles S.S.E.—2 south and 11 S.W. to our station for the night[14]—hoping by this route to fall in with the lodge trace, which Mr. Miller supposes we have left to our right below portage Falls—The bottoms for the first 10 miles were very narrow, but the remainder, up this Fork, are extensive and possess a good soil, except in some few places where they are low and swampy—

Along the hills are a few service-berries, but the prime of their season is past—however wild cherries of various kinds are to be had in the greatest perfection & abundance

Wednesday 9th—On our arrival last evening, I sent Benjamin Jones up the creek, to endeavor, if possible, to find the Indian road, but after walking a considerable distance, he returned without discovering any thing of it, and he says that the tract we had followed all day, but still more to the west—This proving of course totally unfit for our purpose, we this morning crossed the creek, went due east 3 miles, over stony hills, when reaching the main Fork,[15] we followed along the

[12] Camped two miles south-southeast of the site of Inkom, Idaho.
[13] Marsh Creek.
[14] About seven miles south-southeast of the site of McCammon, Idaho.
[15] Portneuf River.

left bank for 7 more, and found a camp and large road, which we took for the one in question—Mr. Miller having, as he supposes, come by a more northerly route and knowing nothing of this spot, we thought it most advisable to continue up the creek,[16] more particularly as lay directly in our course.

3 miles above the Indian Camp, a branch came in from the south, up which a great part of the traces went, and 3 farther on the water again subdivided, the main body ran about north, with a continuation of its cascades, but the small one, which the majority of the trails followed, came from the east: we crossed the latter, and altho' to us an unknown route, trusted to the trace, which in 4 miles brought us to where the branch turned all at once round to S.W.—Here ascending we passed through a gap in the mountains, on the left, which soon brought us to the opposite descent, and discovered an extensive plain lying before us; thro' this we steered due east, and in 18 miles struck a river[17] running through an apparently level country, in *about a south direction,* which Mr. Miller at once pronounced the stream on which he had made his last falls hunt—this river is 100 yards wide, and is here confined between a high rocky bluff bank and a high hill, partially covered with trees of the pine species, but at present appears no more the asylum of the ingenious Beaver than do the bleak summits of the Cordilleras[18]

The prairies being here burnt smooth, we were obliged, tho' now dark, to proceed 2 miles farther ere we could find grass enough to satisfy our hungry horses for the night[19]— having come in all this day 42 miles nearly east—

In the large plain we passed thro', there is considerable fresh sign of Buffalo, which we are in hopes of overtaking in a few days—

[16] Portneuf River.
[17] Bear River.
[18] The Rocky Mountains.
[19] Camped at the site of Soda Springs, Idaho.

Thursday 10*th*—Leaving our station early, we travelled 10 miles E.S.E. and 5 S.E. where, finding an excellent grassy bottom, we stopped for the night,[20] in order to recruit the strength of our horses, which are a good deal jaded by a few of our last days journeys—a plain lodge trace is our guide which follows *up the right bank of this stream,* and shall be our only dependance untill we reach that part Mr. Miller explored—

We saw a number of goats[21] on our march, but have as yet waged an unsuccessful war against them—

Friday 11*th*—We went 6 miles S.E., 2 E.S.E., 2 South & 15 S.S.E. to our encampment,[22] on a small branch issuing from the pine covered mountains on our left, which have in the course of to days journey furnished numberless rills and many runs equal to this, on which we now are—The river meanders in almost every direction, with a gentle current, but the margin is woefully deficient in all kinds of small growth, what little there formerly was having been totally destroyed by the Beaver, nevertheless, a few of these animals still remain, and their principal subsistance are roots & herbs—

A few Antelopes and a good many Geese are the only creatures we get a shot at; a couple of the latter I was fortunate enough to arrest in the course of this days march, and an enormously large black Bear passed in the vicinity of our camp last evening, but altho' we made every exertion, were unable to do him any injury—Our success is bad in the extreme among the land inhabitants, and our almost only resource for food is the produce of our fishing rods from day to day, which is poor Trout and a species of sucker, which is fat and really excellent, called by Virginians the *Stone-toater*—

[20] Seven miles northwest of the site of Georgetown, Idaho.
[21] Antelope.
[22] About four miles north-northwest of the site of Bennington, Idaho.

Saturday 12*th*—Immediately on leaving our last nights station, the country opened very much to the south, the mountains receded to a great distance, and a beautiful low plain occupied the interveening space—8 miles E.S.E. and 6 S.E. brought us to the Forks of the River, where the banks are well supplied with a middling growth of cotton wood—The south branch being considered out of our course, we went along the other 8 miles E. and 1 N.E. making in all 23—[23]

When we returned from drawing our supplies from the water, a number of Indians of the Absaroka, or Crow nation, were at our camp; they behaved decently, and a few returned to their camp to bring us Buffalo meat &ct.

Sunday 13*th*—Knowing the adroitness of these fellows in stealing horses, we doubled our watches, a precaution by no means unnecessary, for having by midnight augmented their numbers to 21, they conducted themselves in such a manner as made it requisite for all of us to keep guard the remainder of the night.—at day break I traded what little meat they had with a few pieces of Buffalo skin, which done, they insisted on selling us horses and demanded gun powder in return.—

This I refused, but they would absolutely exchange some, and at length I acceeded in one instance—Their behaviour was insolent in the extreme, and indicated an evident intention to steal, if not to rob—we kept close possession of our Arms, but notwithstanding our vigilance, they stole a Bag containing the greater part of our kitchen furniture.—to prevent an open rupture, we gave them about twenty loads of Powder & departed, happy at getting off on no worse terms.—Going 10 miles East, over hills, to where a large fork[24] came in from the North, we perceived smokes on several of the highest

[23] About three miles north of the location of Dingle, Idaho.
[24] Thomas Fork.

mountains, in different directions, which concluding to be signals for the purpose of collecting a reinforcement of these
rascals to pursue and attack us, as we could easily discover that
a want of strength, and not of will, was the only thing that
prevented them doing us all possible harm; this morning we
thought it best to vary our former course not only the better
to keep out of their way, but from the information of Mr.
Miller would much sooner reach the part of the country with
which he was acquainted, we left the main stream,[25] and after
following up the right bank of the Fork for 15 miles due north,
encamped on a small branch, having come this day 25 miles—[26]

Monday 14*th*—We unexpectedly passed the night in quiet-
ness, and soon after sunrise continued up the Fork 3 miles,
then ascending the mountains on our right, steered a little to
the W. of north, for 18 more, when we found a considerable
branch running due north,[27] on which we stopped for the
night—[28]

Three Snake Indians came to us in the evening, who, on
hearing that the Absarokas were at no great distance, left
us immediately, in apparent consternation.—

Tuesday 15*th*—Soon after sunrise we were again on horseback, crossed the branch, and continued on for 12 miles N.N.E.
to a low ridge, which passing over, we found another stream,[29]

[25] At this point Stuart departed from what was to become the Oregon
Trail. Only about 110 miles from South Pass as the crow flies, he was about to
begin a detour that, by his reckoning, added over 400 miles. Miller's surmise appears to have been wrong; the party would have reached the country with
which he was familiar if they had continued along the Bear River.

[26] Three miles north-northwest of the site of Geneva, Idaho.

[27] A tributary of Crow Creek, the left fork of Salt River. It may have been
Spring Creek.

[28] About thirteen miles north of the site of Geneva.

[29] Crow Creek.

/1401/

down week to
one
suppod Mad riv.

3 W.

/23/

a greater course of lesser magnitude, and the other much larger, which proves the founder of those, of last falls party, must be Mad river — here I went ... to see whither a passage was practicable in that direction then turned our faces to the west, and at the end of 8 miles, took up our nights quarters in a low point of small cotton woods — Are at last succeeded in killing an antelope which was in fine order, and proved an agreeable addition to our stock of provisions, which is very low —

Friday 18th — Our poor horses having poor employment for their jaws, it was late before we left camp, when proceeding 1 1/2 W.

1½ W.

14 mile west, and ... the ... we have followed these two days, as Jones brought accounts of the impossibility of passing where he went — This ... ... the main body a little below ... the ... of the current became incredible, and ran so close to the mountains as ... ...

/1424/

A page from Stuart's manuscript, September, 1812. The numbers in the margin bracketed by slanted lines are Stuart's; the directions are in an unknown hand.

and went north 15 more, to where it cut through the mountains; here ascending 3 miles E.N.E. brought us to our nights lodgings, on the last water course[30]—saw in the course of the day a multitude of antelopes, but were unsuccessful in procuring meat.—

Wednesday 16th—Our course was 2 miles E.N.E. and 4 N.E. to a large stream[31] running towards the north, which crossing, we found a deep Indian path and followed it for 19 more due north, and encamped[32] on the bank of the river, which runs with great rapidity over a stony and uneaven bed—on striking this water-course, we easily perceived how far we had failed in attaining the object in view, for from all we had learned concerning Miller's River,[33] we ought to have struck it hereabouts, whereas the one we are on runs quite a contrary course and must be a branch of the Snake River—Having thus lost the intended tract by which we proposed crossing the rocky mountains, knowing it must be to the south, and the great probability of falling in again with the Crows, the large Band of whom, did we meet, our Horses would undoubtedly be sacrificed, the other property forcibly taken from us, and our lives perhaps endangered, we at once concluded that our best, safest, and most certain way would be to follow this river down, and pass the first spur of mountains by the route of the party who came across the continent last year.[34]—saw a Black Bear and a great many Antelope, but could not approach either—

[30] To about the location of Fairview, Wyoming.
[31] Salt River.
[32] At about the site of Thayne, Wyoming.
[33] Bear River.
[34] That is, to revert to the original plan by following Hunt's route over Teton Pass.

Thursday 17*th*—Leaving our camp late, we kept at some distance from the right bank of the river, for 11 Miles North, when the path winding to the east, we followed it untill, seeing two streams issuing from the mountains, examined and found the most southerly,[35] a water course of some magnitude, and the other much larger, which from the opinion of those of last fall's party must be Mad river[36]—here I sent Jones to see whether a passage was practicable in that direction, then turned our faces to the west, and at the end of 3 miles, took up our nights quarters,[37] in a low point of small cotton woods—We at last succeeded in killing an Antelope, which was in fine order and proved an agreeable addition to our stock of provisions, which is very low—

Friday 18*th*—Our poor horses having good employment for their jaws, it was late before we left camp, when proceeding 1½ mile west, crossed the Fork we have followed these two days, as Jones brought accounts of the impossibility of passing where he went[38]—This fork joined the main body a little below, when the velocity of the current became incredible and ran so close to the mountains as to compel us to ascend several inferior rises, along an abominable road, caused by the fallen timber and rocks—14½ miles N.W. brought us to where we stopped for the night;[39] the latter part of the way being through Beaver's ponds and quagmires, where our progress was slow indeed, which has been the case the greater part of this days journey.—On the water courses of every size and

[35] Greys River.

[36] The conjecture was correct because Stuart knew the upper Snake by this name.

[37] On the point of land between the Salt and Snake rivers.

[38] Had Jones discovered the route lying along the Snake in the direction of his search, the party could have arrived the following evening at the point not actually reached until October 9.

[39] About six miles north-northwest of the site of Alpine, Idaho.

description which we have seen since we left the crows, the Beavers have by their dams inundated all the low grounds, and are in abundance wherever there is a possibility of their finding a place to live in and a few Willows for their subsistence—

The Indians on many of the small branches attempt to dig them out, but from all appearance they do not succeed to any extent, no doubt from the want of the necessary implements and a little practical knowledge.—

Saturday 19*th*—We were all up at dawn, and I had just reached the river bank when I heard the Indian yell raised in the vicinity of our camp and the cry, "To Arms" there are Indians, echoed by all of our party—We had just time to snatch our arms when several Indians at full speed passed 300 yards to one side of our stations, having by their yells driven off every horse we had (notwithstanding their being tethered & hobbled); towards them we rushed, and got almost within shot of the nearest, when repeated yells in the direction from which they came made us desist from the pursuit in order to defend ourselves and baggage, for their being only a few Indians after the horses, we very readily imagined that the main body were in reserve to attack our rear, did we follow the foremost, or to plunder the Camp, if opportunity.—

At the rate the horses were going, all attempts to regain them would be unavailing, and had we pursued farther, every thing else should have been lost to a certainty, which would have undoubtedly have made our situation, if possible, far more deplorable than it really is—The savages whose yells made us return to the baggage passed soon after in the others tracks, and we could not discover that the whole party amounted to more than 20, which had we known only 3 minutes sooner, a few horses might probably have been saved

& a scalp or two fallen into our hands—From a few words we heard, they are beyond all doubt of the Crow nation and, I believe, the band we met at Millers river.—

This method of stealing horses is deserving of being more minutely described; one of the party rode past our camp and placed himself on a conspicuous knob, in the direction they wanted to run them off; when the others (who were hidden behind our camp), seeing him prepared, rose the warwhoop, or yell (which is the most horribly discordant howling imaginable, being in imitation of the different beasts of prey); at this diabolical noise, the animals naturally rose their heads to see what the matter was—at that instant he who had planted himself in advance put spurs to his steed, and ours, seeing him gallop off in apparent fright, started all in the same direction, as if a legion of infernals were in pursuit of them.—In this manner a dozen or two of these fellows have sometimes succeeded in running off every horse belonging to our parties, of perhaps 5 or 600 men; for once those creatures take fright, nothing short of broken necks, can stop their progress.—

On the whole this was one of the most daring, and intrepid actions I ever heard of among Indians, and convinces me how determined they were on having our horses, for which they would unquestionably have followed us any distance, and nothing but seeing us prepared and ready to defend ourselves prevented their attacking us where we first saw them—

We have been busy all day, making preparations to set out in the morning on foot down the river, along the plains of which, below Henry's Fort, we have hopes of meeting with some of the Snakes, from whom if we can procure a couple of horses, we shall continue our former determination, and if possible, reach the Cheyenne river before the winter sets in, but should we fail in this, our winter quarters will probably be some where on the Spanish river[40]—we have just food

[40] Green River.

enough for one meal and rely with confidence on the inscrutable ways of providence to send in our road wherewith to subsist on from day to day—

Sunday 20*th*—Last night, Jones set our old Beaver Trap, (the only one we have) and caught a middle sized Beaver.— It was 10 A.M. before we were ready to depart, when collecting every article we could not carry, committed to the flames whatever would consume and the remainder we threw into the river; resolved to prevent the villans benefiting more by us—for two of the same band were (by Jones) seen this morning, sculking near our camp, in order, no doubt, to observe where we should deposit what part of our effects we could not carry—

We went on for 10 miles N.W. when, finding a good fishing place, we stoped for the night,[41] and 40 Trout were taken by dusk—We took with us only what was thought absolutely necessary, but we find our bundles very heavy, and the road is by no means a dead level—

Monday 21*st*—we set out early, and going along the river, found a Beaver in our Trap, which we took out and cut up, in order that each might carry his share.—after walking 8 miles N.W. we stopped for the purpose of making rafts to cross the River,[42] as wood appears scarce below, and it is no where fordable—Forty five Trout were the produce of Mr. Millers and my fishing rods, but they are poor and very indifferent food; and were it not for the little meat we occasionally fall in with, I really think they would not even support life—

[41] About ten miles southeast of the location of Irwin, Idaho.

[42] Stuart may have intended to turn east at this point. If so, he was already planning to traverse Teton Pass, rather than go north to Henry's Fort for horses.

Tuesday 22nd—The rafts were ready, and we embarked on them at 10 A.M., three on the one and four on the other; after going thro' some very rough and strong water, found them safe and steady, which, instead of crossing, induced us to continue on for 20 miles N.W. when we encamped on a beautiful low point[43] and hauled up our *flat bottoms* to dry—

In the evening going to set the Trap, Jones killed a Fallow Deer and a Wolverine,[44] which is the more fortunate, as we can carry the meat on our rafts.—

Wednesday 23rd—In addition to the produce of Jones' hunt yesternight, Vallée caught a large Beaver in the Trap and shot another, which was so fat that it sunk before he could get to the spot.—We embarked late and went 10 miles N.W. 2 N.E. 6 N.W. 1 N. & 1 N.E., which brought us to our nights station early,[45] having nearly upset one of our rafts a little way above and got all our Arms &ct. wet—The river is very rapid and full of Beaver; we might have shot several in the course of the day, but thought it a pity, as we have meat enough for the present—

Thursday 24th—It was late before every thing was dry and shipped; 4 miles N.W. brought us to a part of the river where the mountains on the right and cut bluffs on the left made us apprehensive of rapids, impassable for our craft, being at no great distance; we therefore stopped, and on examination found the water good, except in one place, where, to preserve our bundles from getting wet, we unloaded and made a short portage—12 miles farther on, we came to a little island, where

[43] At a spot east by north from the site of Iona, Idaho.

[44] A badger?

[45] Due west from the location of Ucon, Idaho, and somewhat north of the middle of the great bend made by the river in this area.

were some Elk, one of which, on being wounded, took to the water and drifted a mile before we overtook and hauled it a shore, where on account of strong appearances of bad weather, we stopped for the night.[46]—the last 3 miles were in about a N.E. direction—

Friday 25*th*—On skinning the Elk, a Ball and an Arrow point were found in its body, which to all appearance must have been in it about a week—This leads us to believe that the Blackfeet were here not long since and were the persons who wounded it—The meat proved very good, and we remained here all day, drying it—Rain, hail and at last snow fell in the course of the afternoon and evening.

Saturday 26*nd*—Rain fell during the greater part of the night; at a late hour we embarked every thing, and at the end of one mile N.N.W. put a short on the left bank, for the purpose of completing the drying of our Elk, and adding some logs to our rafts, as the additional weight of meat sinks them too deep to proceed with safety—

Sunday 27*th*—Our rafts were ready about sunset, and we set off early this morning; our course was, I believe, from every point of the compass, for 32 miles when, having advanced considerably into the low plain on the left, and the mountains on the right being now reduced to moderate sized hills, we stopped on the left bank for the night,[47] intending to cross the river in the morning and proceed on foot—

Monday 28*th*—We remained in the same camp all this day, making mogasins and other preparations for our journey—

[46] Twenty-five miles south of the site of Newdale, Idaho.
[47] Two miles north-northeast of the site of Ririe, Idaho.

Before sunset our meat, about 20 lbs. each, was divided, and every thing else in readiness to cross the river early, and proceed by plains to the south of Henry's Fort.—

Mad river is generally a very rapid stream, from 1 to 200 yards wide, winds about in every direction among the mountains, which are of great magnitude on the east, but deserve no other name than hills on the west—Its banks are principally composed of gravel, occasionally indeed a thin soil covers this, but is partial, even in the same bottom—The body of the mountains and hills is a hard black rock, the former produce a great number of the pine species and some red cedars, but the latter are little else than barrens, with a growth of small stunted grass—

Immense quantities of Beaver inhabit mad river and its tributary streams, & wherever the soil is in the least propitious, a great abundance of small cotton woods and willow are every where to be found for their support—

Though this watercourse runs with incredible velocity, it is (so far as I can judge from information and observation) entirely free from either Falls, cascades, or bad rapids, and is generally confined in one body untill it here extricates itself from the mountains and divides into innumerable channels, making islands without number, all covered with some kind of wood and equally the resort of Beaver in multitudes—

Tuesday 29*th*—Crossed the river early, and after traversing an extensive Bottom of Cotton Wood, Hawthorn, and Willow, ascended the upper bank and went 15 miles N.E. over very rough ground, where we encamped on a small branch[48] in the hills, very much fatigued—

Saw three antelopes, but thought it imprudent to shoot

[48] On Moody Creek, at a point about fourteen miles west of the location of Sam, Idaho.

at them, as it is more than probable the Blackfeet are in the vicinity, and should they discover us, inevitable destruction must be our lot—

Wednesday 30*th*—We yesterday fell in with a large trace made by horses, apparently about 3 weeks ago, but of what nation cannot as yet tell; we are however inclined to believe they were absarokas, come here probably to see whether an establishment had been made in this neighborhood, which, from what Mr. Hunt told them last year, they had every reason to expect—They had encamped on this branch, which their road crossed a little higher and lay in our course for 2 miles, when it separated in every direction and we lost it—our course was the same as yesterday, and 19 miles more brought us to our nights lodgings,[49] in a deep gully—Mr. Crooks had been somewhat indisposed for two days, and this evening has a very alarming fever.—A little to one side of our camp, one of the Canadians (in searching for good water) discovered several very astonishing springs of various qualities and temperatures, some of them are cold, others hot: one of the cold we found to be aciduated and impregnated in a small degree with iron; but the principal one in the group is very hot & sulphuric, the water is oily to the touch and foams like soap suds; its margin is covered with a yellow efflorescence of sulphur, which affects the sense of smelling at some distance, and the volume of smoke that issues immediately from this spring may be distinguished at least two miles off.—

[49] On Canyon Creek, about thirteen miles west of the location of Tetonia, Idaho.

[October 1812]

Thursday October 1st—At an early hour we ascended the hill, where Mr. McClellan, to whose lot it had fallen to carry the Trap, refused to be its bearer any longer, neither would he pack an equivalent in dried meat, but leaving us, said he could kill enough for his daily subsistence, and when informed we would cross the mountain to the right, the better to avoid the Blackfeet in whose walks we now were, his answer was that he must consult the case of his sore feet, and went on around the base.—

We reached the other side by the middle of the afternoon, and found the passage of the mountain somewhat difficult on account of the snow, which in many places was of considerable depth.—Mr. McClellan was seen a head of us, in the plain below, as we were descending—6 miles from its base we reached a river 50 yards wide, and about knee deep, with abundance of willow & Beaver—[1]

The plain, from the mountain we traversed today to the pilot knobs,[2] is about 19 miles in width, and the river running through it falls into Henrys River, half way between his Fork

[1] Teton River.
[2] The Teton Mountains.

and the mouth of mad River—the whole of this days march was 18 miles E.S.E.—[3]

Mr. Crooks' indisposition encreased so much this afternoon that I insisted on his taking a dose of Castor oil, which fortunately had the desired effect, but he has such a violent fever and is withal so weak as to preclude all idea of continuing our journey untill his recovery—notwithstanding the urgent solicitations of my men to proceed without him; very justly representing the imminent dangers we exposed ourselves to by any delay in the unknown and barren tract, among most inveterate enemies to whites and in the midst of impervious mountains of snow at such an advanced season, without one days provision, and no very favourable appearances of procuring an addition here, did we even venture to hunt—Such a prospect I must confess made an impression on my mind that cannot easily be described, but the thoughts of leaving a fellow creature in such a forlorn situation were too repugnant to my feelings to require long deliberation, particularly as it was probable he might get well in a few days; this hope I suggested and at length prevailed on them, tho' very reluctantly to abide the event—

The sensations excited on this occasion and by the view of an unknown & untravelled wilderness are not such as arise in the artificial solitude of parks and gardens, for there one is apt to indulge a flattering notion of self sufficiency, as well as a placid indulgence of voluntary delusions; whereas the phantoms which haunt a desert are want, misery, and danger, the evils of dereliction rush upon the mind; man is made unwillingly acquainted with his own weakness, and meditation shows him only how little he can sustain and how little he can perform—

[3] Camp was on the river and about three miles west southwest of the site of Tetonia. By turning south the next morning Stuart revealed another change in plan: he was now aiming for Teton Pass rather than Henry's Fort.

Friday 2nd—Jones, in searching for a place to set the Trap, met a White Bear,[4] which he was obliged to fire at in self defence, but only wounding him, he made his escape—Mr. Crooks is rather easier, but unable to move or take any food, therefore, not knowing how long we may be detained here, however disagreeable and dangerous—I sent Jones out early, in quest of game, who in about two hours returned, having killed five Elk; we immediately moved forward (supporting Mr. Crooks) for 6 miles south, up the creek, to where the dead animals lay, and encamped in the vicinity[5]—the weather for some days past, has been principally cold.—

Sunday 4th—Mr. Crooks continued both yesterday and to day too weak and feverish to proceed; we had no more medecine, but had recourse to an Indian sweat, which appears to have a good effect, and we are in great hopes of being able to move on again to morrow—

Saturday 5th—By carrying Mr. Crooks' things, we were enabled to go on 8 miles, for the most part through swamps, in a southerly direction, where finding some good fire wood and an excellent camp, we stopped for the night[6]—Several branches issue from the Pilot knob mountains on the east, which, on reaching the low grounds, are dammed up by Beaver and occasion the swamps through which we passed to day— On our way here, we killed a white Bear, which had 3½ inches fat on the rump, and proves an agreeable addition to our stock of Elk meat—

---

[4] Grizzly bear.
[5] About five miles west of the site of Driggs, Idaho.
[6] About five miles southwest of the site of Driggs.

Tuesday 6th We set out early, and leaving the swamps on our right, proceeded along the mountain, through the plain 13 miles S.S.E. where the main body of the river issuing from the Pilot Knobs, we ascended it 4 miles S.E. and encamped where it divides nearly into equal branches[7]—Mr. C. mends slowly and was able to carry his Rifle & Pistol for the most part of to day—

Wednesday 7th—We continued on, up the right hand Fork[8] for 13 miles S.E. by E. to the summit of the Pilot Knob mountain,[9] on which we found about nine inches snow—9 miles same course brought us to mad river, and in 2 more reached the opposite bank, having crossed five channels, of from 30 to 60 yds. wide each and from 2 to 3½ feet water, a very rapid current, and in every other respect of the same character as the part we descended on the rafts, with the exception that the valley is here several miles wide, and some of the bottoms upwards a mile broad and thickly covered with better cotton woods and Pines—[10]

Thursday 8th—6 miles S.S.E. brought us to a considerable path along the hills. 6 S.S.W. was our next course, down to where mad River enters the mountains, when ascending a high hill, went 11 more E.S.E. and encamped on a small branch,[11] there being good sign of Beaver—saw a great many Antelopes, but did not succeed in killing any, although we had not a mouthful to eat—

[7] Close to the site of Victor, Idaho.
[8] Trail Creek.
[9] Teton Pass.
[10] Three miles west of the location of Jackson, Wyoming.
[11] Horse Creek, which enters about ten miles south of the site of Jackson.

Friday 9th—In 6 miles S.E. we reached Hoback's fork, a stream about 50 yards wide, with a good body of water, which runs to the west and joins Mad River some distance below; we next proceeded up the Fork 6 miles East, when killing an Antelope, we encamped immediately, though early in the day —It was a buck and very poor, but with a Beaver which Vallée killed some distance below, it made tolerable eating; at least we found it so, having ate nothing since we breakfasted on a few poor Trout and a small Duck yesterday morning—

Saturday 10th—Our route to day was 6 miles up the Fork, to Cross Creek[12] 20 yards wide—3 to Henry's hill[13]—2 up the small branch, where the side of the mountain, having been precipitated from the main body, has partly stopped the channel of the *run*, and made a pond upwards of 300 feet in circumference, very deep, and the residence of some Beaver— 3½ miles over a mountain brought us again to Hobach's Fork, which following for 4½ more, we reached Hunters Fork,[14] and encamped between that and the main stream,[15] having come 19 miles nearly due East, the greatest part along an abominable road, occasioned by the proximity of the mountains, where the track is in some places so nearly perpendicular that missing a single step you would go several hundred feet into the rocky bed of the stream below—

Sunday 11th—We ate the remainder of our old Buck meat, and went on at a smart pace 10 miles S.East, where taking up a small branch, in 9 more east found where Mr. McClellan had encamped and supped upon the carcase of a poor wolf the

[12] Granite Creek.
[13] Game Hill.
[14] Jack Creek.
[15] Close to the site of Bondurant, Wyoming.

night before: being as near the spanish river mountain[16] as we could find water, and the day too far advanced to ascend it, we stopped at the same place,[17] and went to bed without supper—

Monday 12*th*—At the dawn we resumed our journey, and continued on for 2 miles to the base of the mountain, the ascent of which is steep and difficult; about noon, we reached the drains of the spanish River, and by the middle of the afternoon, struck the main body, a stream about 160 yards wide, with no great depth of water, no timber, and but few Willows—Here we expected to find Buffalo in abundance, but a few old Bulls tracks were all we had for hope, except a few Antelopes on the brow of the mountain, which were so wild as to preclude all hopes of getting near them—Our course was E.S.E. 16 miles, to the river, which crossing, we followed its left bank for 11 more S.W. in quest of Beaver sign, which we at length found, and encamped in the vicinity[18] —saw a large smoke at some distance to the N.W. and sent Leclaire to see what occasioned it: we had great hopes of its being Indians, consequently sat up late, waiting his return, in expectation of getting something to eat, but at last despairing of his coming, we went to bed about midnight, again supperless, but in hopes of our old Trap procuring us something for breakfast.—

Tuesday 13*th*—We were up with the dawn, and visited our Trap with anxious expectation, but found nothing in it, except the forepaw of a Beaver; which has greatly depressed our spirits; not feeling in very good trim to resume our jour-

---

[16] Not a true mountain but a high ridge running north and south along the Green River.

[17] About twenty miles north of the present town of Daniel, Wyoming.

[18] About seventeen miles north-northeast of the location of Daniel.

ney, but there being no alternative, we started, and soon after met Leclaire coming up the river with information that the smoke was occasioned by Mr. McClellan's camp taking fire, while he was at some little distance fishing, but without success—he informed Leclaire of his having been very much indisposed, and lived on little or nothing, ever since he parted with us; that he was happy of our being near (as well he might) and would wait our arrival at his camp, in hopes we should have something for him to eat, without which he could not proceed much farther: on our getting to him, he was lying on a parcel of straw, emaciated and worn to a perfect skeleton, hardly able to raise his head or speak from extreme debility, but our presence seemed to revive him considerably—and by a good deal of persuasion, we prevailed on him to accompany us, but with apparent reluctance, saying it was as well for him to die there as any where else, there being no prospect of our getting any speedy relief; we carried all his things, and proceeded on for 17 miles S.E. over a level barren of sand and to a small branch, where we encamped early,[19] on account of seeing a few antelopes in the neighborhood—soon after stopping, we all made an unsuccessful attempt to procure some meat, and after dark returned to camp with heavy hearts, but we could not in justice enter the same complaint against our stomachs—

As we were preparing for bed, one of the Canadians advanced towards me, with his Rifle in his hand, saying that as there was no appearance of our being able to procure any provisions at least untill we got to the extreme of this plain, which would require 3 or 4 days, he was determined to go no farther; but that lots should be cast and one die to save the rest, that I should be exempted in consequence of being their leader &ct.—

I shuddered at the idea, and used every endeavor to cre-

[19] About eleven miles north of the site of Daniel.

ate an abhorrence in his mind against such an act; urging also the probability of our falling in with some animal on the morrow; but finding that my argument failed, and that he was on the point of converting some others to his purpose—I snatched up my Rifle, cocked, and leveled it at him, with the firm resolution to fire if he persisted; this so terrified the fellow, that he fell instantly on his knees and asked the whole parties pardon, solemnly swearing he should never again suggest such a thought—

after this affair was settled, my thoughts began to ruminate on our hapless & forlorn situation with the prospects before us: untill I at length became so agitated and weak that it was with difficulty I crawled to bed, and after being there, I (for the first time in my life) could not enjoy that repose my exhausted frame so much wanted; this naturally led my revery to a retrospective view of former happy days, when troubles, difficulties, and distress were to me only things imaginary, which now convinces one how little a man who rolls in affluence, and knows neither cares nor sorrows, can feel for those of others, and he undoubtedly of all people in the world is least qualified for pious deeds—

Let him visit these regions of want and misery; his riches will prove an eye sore, and he will be taught the pleasure and advantage of prayer—If the advocates for the rights of man come here, they can enjoy them, for this is the land of *liberty and equality*, where a man sees, and feels, that he is a man merely, and that he can no longer exist than while he can himself procure the means of support.—

Wednesday 14*th*—We resumed our line of march a little before day light, and went on but slowly for 9 miles S.East, when we came to the base of some hills, which we ascended, going nearly east, and had scarcely proceeded 2 miles when to our great joy we discovered an old run down Buffalo Bull, which after considerable trouble we succeeded in killing about 2 P.M. —and so ravenous were our appetites, that we ate part of the animal raw; then cut up the most of what was eatable and carried it to a brook at some little distance,[20] where we encamped, being hungry enough to relish a hearty meal—

Thursday 15th—We sat up the greater part of the night, eating and barbecueing meat: I was very much alarmed at the voracious manner in which all ate, but happily none felt any serious inconvenience therefrom—probably in consequence of my not allowing them to eat freely before they had supped a quantity of broth—Being somewhat recruited and refreshed by the middle of the day, we left camp, with the intention of going down this river so long as it lies in our course, or at least to the point of a mountain[21] we see in the east, near which we expect to find the Missouri waters: In 12 miles E.S.E. over low hills, struck a bend of the river,[22] and stopped for the night—

We this day crossed a large Indian trail, about 15 days old, steering nearly a N.E. course, which we suppose must have been made by the crows, who (from the numerous skeletons of Buffaloe we find in every direction) must have hunted in this country the most part of the summer: We have seen only a few goats, which were exceedingly wild—

Friday 16th—By sunrise we left the River, which here ran to the West of south, when passing over a low ridge, found a

[20] According to the journal kept by Stuart while making the journey, the party stayed in camp during the fourteenth, a statement that is confirmed by a check of directions and distances. This campsite was therefore the same as that occupied on the thirteenth.

[21] One of the Wind River Mountains.

[22] Actually New Fork River. They encamped about where this river crosses the 110th meridian.

flat, extending to the foot of the mountains on our left, with a Willow Branch meandering through it, which we crossed soon after—15 miles from last nights station, we forded another stream, of considerable magnitude, whose banks were adorned with many Pines—near which we found an Indian encampment of large dimensions, deserted apparently about a month ago, with immense numbers of Buffalo bones strewed every where in the neighborhood—

In the centre of this camp is a Lodge 150 feet in circumference, composed of, or rather supported by, 20 trees, 12 inches in diameter and 44 feet long; across these were branches of Pine and Willow laid, so as to make a tolerable shade—

At the west end and immediately opposite the door, three persons lay interred, with their feet toward the east; at the head of each was a branch of red cedar, firmly inserted in the ground, and a large Buffalo's scull painted black placed close by the root of each—This building is circular, and from the quantity and size of the materials must have required great labour and time in erection, from which we infer that the personages on whose account it was constructed were not of the common order; on many parts of it were suspended numerous ornaments, and among the rest, a great number of children's mogasins—9 miles farther on, we reached another creek, equal in size to the last, with a few cotton woods and many Willows —here we encamped,[23] having come 24 miles E.S.E.—

Saturday 17*th*—5 miles from last nights station is a large creek, and 7 farther on is another, with a great many Willows and a few trees of Pine and Cotton-wood—It is very shallow, and like the others we have lately crossed, runs to the west south, with a considerable range of hills along its left bank—all these Creeks are tributary streams of the Spanish River, and take

[23] About six miles north by west from the site of Boulder, Wyoming.

their rise in the ridge of mountains to the east, which is the main range of the rocky mountains, it is stupenduously high and rugged, composed of huge masses of a blackish coloured rock, almost totally destitute of timber, and covered in many places with snow—Our journey to day was 12 miles E.S.E.[24] saw a few Bulls and many Antelopes, but could not kill any— Our living is of the meanest kind, being poor Bull meat and Buck antelope, both too bad to be eat, except in cases of starvation—

Sunday 18*th*—Soon after crossing the ridge which lay before us, we found the stream we encamped on last night, coming from the S.E. Wading it, we proceeded thro' a low plain, till having gone 12 miles S.E. struck it again, and on ascending the opposite bank, met about 130 Indians of the snake nation —They were encamped on the creek, and by accompanying them 3 miles N.E. we reached their huts,[25] which were 40 in number, made principally of pine branches; they were poor but hospitable in the extreme, and for a Pistol, a Breech cloth, an axe, a knife, a Tin Cup, two Awls, and a few Beads, they gave us the only horse they had, the Crows in their late excursion through this country having deprived them of all these Animals, as well as of a number of their Women &ct.; for a few Trinkets, we got some Buffalo meat and leather mogasins, an article we much want—

They informed us that the crows had fallen in with two of our hunters last spring, and robbed them of every thing, which the poor fellows opposed and in the fray killed 7 savages, but were at last overpowered and massacred—They also told us that two of the Canadians left by Mr. Crooks last Winter had early in the spring accompanied one of their bands

[24] On East Fork River, about seven miles east of the site of Boulder.
[25] About seven miles northeast of the location of Big Sandy, Wyoming.

to hunt Buffalo on the head waters of the Missouri, where they, as well as many of their people, were killed by the Blackfeet: —It undoubtedly was those two unfortunate wretches who conducted the Indians to our Caches on the Snake River—[26]

Last summer, they said, that the Arapahays fell in with Champlain,[27] and 3 men he had hunting Beaver, some distance down the spanish River, murdered them in the dead of the night and took possession of all their effects—

When we told them the day was not far distant when we should take signal vengeance on the perpetrators of those deeds, they appeared quite elated, and offered their services in the execution, which were of course accepted, and a long smoke, out of the Calumet of Peace, ended the conference—

These fellows have a kind of wild Tobacco, which grows spontaneously in the plains adjacent to the spanish River Mountains, the leaves are smaller than those of ours, and it is much more agreeable, not being nearly so violent in its effects —These mountains, which my *hungry spell* prevented me from noticing in due order, are principally composed of pumice stone, granate, Flint &ct. there is a species of clay, which is very fine and light, of an agreeable smell, and of a brown colour, spotted with yellow, dissolves readily in the mouth, and like all those kinds of earth, adheres strongly to the tongue; the natives manufacture jars, pots, and dishes of different descriptions from it; these vessels, communicate a very pleasant smell and flavour to the water, &ct. that is put in them, which undoubtedly proceeds from the solution of some bituminous substance contained in the clay: there are also several

---

[26] On his westward journey of the previous year Hunt had left St. Michel, Delauney, Detayé, and Carson in the mountains to trap. Detayé was killed by the Crows while the four were on their way to the headwaters of the Missouri River. But the three who had conducted the Shoshones to the caches were La Chapelle, Landry, and Turcotte, French-Canadians who had become discouraged and returned to the Snake River area.

[27] Jean Baptiste Champlain. His death occurred on the Arkansas River.

kinds of metallic earths, or chalks, of various colours, such as green, Blue, yellow, Black, White, and two kinds of ochre, the one pale and the other a bright red, like vermillion, these are held in high estimation by the natives and neighboring Tribes, who use them to paint their bodies and faces, which they do in a very fanciful manner.—

Monday 19*th*—By sunrise we had our old horse loaded with meat sufficient for 5 days, and proceeded 3 miles south, over very rough ground, which brought us into the (large) Crow trace, along which not less than 100 lodges must have passed —We followed this road 12 miles S.E. to a creek coming from the east, then crossing, went 3 E.S.E. up a low ridge, and in 3 more, keeping that course, we found the last stream again, running through a large flat covered with willow—The wind blew cold from the N.E. with some snow that made us think of encamping, and by going down the creek 1 mile, we found an eligible place—[28]

Tuesday 20*th*—Vallée and Leclaire killed a young Bull (last evening), which was in very good order—some snow fell in the night, which made it late before we set out, when pursuing a S.E. course for 18 miles thro' a beautifully undulating country, having the main mountain on the left and a considerably elevated ridge on the right—

The ridge of mountains,[29] which divides Wind river from the columbia and spanish waters, ends here abruptly, and winding to the North of east, becomes the separator of a branch of big horn and Cheyenne Rivers from the other water courses which add their waves to the Missouri below the Sioux country—

[28] Ten miles east-southeast of the site of Big Sandy.
[29] The Wind River Mountains.

On the Spanish River, as far as we could see yesterday, the country appeared to be almost a dead level, bounded to the west by a range of very high mountains, running about S.W., and on the east by the ridge to the right of the country thro' which we passed to day, which keeps a course about S.S.W.—

We abandoned the Crow trace early in the day, as it bore to the North of east, and being somewhat apprehensive of falling in with some of their spies, for, according to the information received from the snakes, they are on a river at no great distance to the east, and we suppose ourselves now at the source of the Spanish River waters in this quarter.

Our right hand ridge becoming very low, we passed over into a low plain, and 8 miles S.S.E. brought us to camp,[30] on a little drain in the bare prairie, where our fuel was an indifferent growth of sage, which proving an unsuccessful competitor against the piercing northeaster of this evening, we were obliged to take refuge in our nest at an early hour—In the plain we traversed today are several springs of clear and limpid water, which overflows the surface and becomes crystalized into a salt as white as snow—

This valley is about 10 miles in circumference, and is entirely covered, for the depth of a foot to 18 inches, with a crust of salt, which is collected by the natives, who are excessively fond of it, while those near the sea hold it in abhorrence, and will eat nothing that has in the least been touched thereby—

The surrounding mountains, as far as I could discover, afford no indication of mineral Salt, but they must necessarily abound with it, from the great quantities deposited by these springs—

[30] Five miles southwest of the entrance to South Pass.

Wednesday 21st—Mr. McClellan killed some Buffalo last evening, to get some of which we waited this morning—The cold continued, and was accompanied by snow, soon after we left the drain, which compelled us to encamp, at the end of 15 miles E.N.E., on the side of a lofty mountain,[31] which we must inevitably traverse—We found a sufficiency of dry aspen for firewood; but not a drop of water—about 2 miles back we crossed a large Lodge trace, steering a little to the right of the point of the mountain; this, as well as the other trails we have lately crossed, must have been made by another band of the Crows, who may have been hunting lower down on the spanish river.

Thursday 22nd—We set out at day light, and ascended about 3 miles, when we found a spring of excellent water, and breakfasted; 5 more brought us to the top of the mountain, which we call the *big horn*,[32] it is in the midst of the principal chain; in scrambling up the acclivity and on the top, we discovered various shells, evidently the production of the sea, and which doubtless must have been deposited by the waters of the deluge—

The summit of this mountain,[33] whose form appears to be owing to some volcanic eruption, is flat, and exhibits a plain of more than 3 miles square; in the middle is a considerable Lake,[34] which from every appearance was formerly the crater of a volcano; the principal chain of these mountains is situ-

[31] At the western end of South Pass.

[32] This elevation bears no name today.

[33] Here Stuart was on the Continental Divide. That morning he had elected to climb the ridge on which he now stood, rather than turning north up the ascent that led to the summit of South Pass. His present position gave him another opportunity to descend to the Sweetwater River and the route that was to be followed by the emigrant trains. But because lack of information forced him to make his decisions solely on the basis of what he could see, he led his party down the south slope to the level plain below.

[34] Neither plain nor lake has been discovered.

ated between four of less height that are parallel to it; these lateral chains are generally about 40 or 50 miles distant from the principal, but are connected with it, in several places, by transverse spurs or ramifications; from these ridges many other branches extend outwardly, composed of small mountains occasionally running in different directions—

12 miles more brought us to the base of the mountain, where we found a little water oozing out of the earth; it was of a whitish colour, and possessed a great similarity of taste to the muddy watches of the missouri—

Here we encamped,[35] having come 20 miles E. by south, We saw a number of Ibex,[36] or big horn, and killed two, which we find excellent eating—

Friday 23rd—The morning was piercingly cold, but immediately after an early breakfast we continued on for 7 miles E.S.E. which brought us to the head drains of a water course, running east, among banks and low hills of a loose, bluish coloured earth, apparently strongly impregnated with Copperas: supposing this a water of the Missouri, we intend to follow its banks—For a few miles it ran east, but turning gradually to S. by West, we left it, and steered S.E. in hopes of falling in with a bend of it—Ascending a hill at the end of 26 miles, we saw the creek at a considerable distance, running about S.S.E., and the country in every direction South of east is a plain, bounded only by the horizon; we at once concluded to give up all idea of taking the creek for our guide, and to make the best of our way for a range of mountains in the east, about 60 miles off, near which we are in great hopes of finding another stream, and have determined on wintering at the first eligible place—This hill we called discovery knob,

[35] About eighteen miles south-southeast of the site of Atlantic City.
[36] Probably antelope, in spite of their being called "big horn."

which leaving, we separated in quest of water, and were fortunate enough to find a few puddles in the high prairie, about 1 ½ mile due north—here we had to encamp[37] without a single stick of firewood—

Saturday 24th—The wind blew excessively cold from the north east, which compelled us to decamp before the dawn; 27 Miles E. by north was the length of this days journey,[38] over tolerably level ground of very indifferent quality; a march truly disagreeable, being greatly annoyed by a heavy snow, which accompanied the high wind for several hours, we travelled untill very late in the day in hopes of finding water, but seeing no appearance of it, we at length contented ourselves, with snow as a substitute, and had no other fuel than Buffalo Dung—

Sunday 25th—This day on the whole was mild and pleasant, found a small brook, a few miles from last nights station, when we breakfasted, and after travelling 32 miles east, encamped[39] after dusk, with but little fuel and no water—Saw a very lofty range of snowy mountains in the South, running east & west—

a great many Buffalo have lately travelled thro' this country, and a few were seen at no great distance from us to day, but in consequence of getting the wind of us, they scampered before we could approach near enough to do execution—

Our poor old horse is almost done out, for want of two very material necessaries—Grass and Water, the latter in particular we have been very scantily supplied with for several days back—

[37] About thirty-eight miles north of the present town of Tipton, Wyoming.

[38] To the point about three miles west of the right angle formed by Lost Creek.

[39] Five miles west of the present town of Bairoil, Wyoming.

Monday 26*th*—We went 5 miles by the dawn, when having passed a low gap to the right of the mountain, on a drain running E.S.E. we found water, and halted a couple of hours; after breakfasting at this place, we renewed our march for 9 more, where seeing the channel of this stream turn due south, without a drop of water running over its sandy bed, we quitted it without hesitation, and steered E.N.E. for a wooded ravine in another mountain, at a small distance from the base of which, we, to our great joy, discovered a Creek (with muddy banks, and a great abundance of Willow) running N.N.W. with a considerable body of water, here we stopped for the night,[40] having come to day 14 Miles E S E and 13 E.N.E.

Tuesday 27*th*—Jones caught a Beaver last night, and early this morning two Bulls that straggled near camp were put to death, on account of which, and feeding ourselves, as well as our horse, pretty much fatigued, we remained in the same camp all day—

Wednesday 28*th*—Making an early start, we followed the right bank of the Creek, 10 miles N.N.W. when it turned abruptly to N.E by E., breaking thro' a range of hills into a handsome plain, when meandering still more to the north, we steered E.N.East, and stopped for the night,[41] on its bank, at the end of 17 miles—here the creek, which at last nights station was scarcely 10 wide, has increased to the breadth of 20 yards, which accumulation of water, excepting two little rivulets from the south west, joined the branch we descended, about 3 miles above this, from nearly a north direction—

[40] On Muddy Creek, at the entrance of Muddy Gap.

[41] On the Sweetwater River three miles below the mouth of Muddy Creek. Stuart here returned to the route that was to become the Oregon Trail.

Tuesday 29*th*—The river, after running 3 miles nearly south, forced a passage[42] through a high range of hills, covered with cedars, into an extensive low country, affording excellent pasture for the numerous herds of Buffalo with which it abounded —We killed three cows this morning, which are the first we have been able to lay our paws on; the hump meat is by far the most delicious I have ever tasted—after following the river 17 miles E.N.E. we encamped[43] among a few large white willows—To the North the plain is bounded by low bare ridges, but towards the south they are much higher, very rugged, and covered with a few Cedars—

Friday 30*th*—Considerable snow fell during the night, however, we renewed our march at an early hour—In the afternoon, finding that the river ran to the south, we crossed it, ascended the opposite heights, and went along them some distance till the hour of encamping being at hand, without any prospect of getting water in the highlands, we descended a deep ravine, thickly wooded with scrubby Cedars, in hopes of reaching the stream every moment, but to our surprise the way became impassible for our horse, which obliged us to leave him, and we continued on a few hundred yards,[44] where the stream is reduced to one half of what it was; where we crossed, it is confined between red coloured precipices of stone, at least 500 feet high—the bed of the river was composed of huge masses of rock, and the current dashing over them with the most violent impetuousity—to form somewhat of an adequate idea, let one imagine numerous streams pouring from the mountains into one channel, struggling for expansion in a narrow passage, exasperated by rocks rising in their way,

42 Devil's Gate.
43 Nearly opposite Independence Rock.
44 Here Stuart first encountered the North Platte River.

and at last discharging all their violence of water by a sudden fall thro' the horrid chasm—The wind was cold, and we took refuge for the night,[45] among the Cedars, having come to day 34 Miles E.N.E.—

Light was the supper of our fourfooted companion, and not a drop of water to slacken his or our thirst, till Leclaire, with considerable danger to himself, succeeded in procuring us enough for a drink each—

Saturday 31*st*—We resumed our march early, and were obliged to go considerably out of our way on account of the bluffs, which extended much farther into the interior than we had any idea of—We saw many Buffalo in the high plains, and numerous flocks of Ibex and black Tailed Deer in the Bluff ravines, which were for the most part composed of a loose white earth, with partial patches of stunted Cedars along their sides—We came at last to a place where we could over-look the river, and saw a channel torn through red piles of rocks, by which the stream is obstructed and broken till it comes to a very deep descent, of such dreadful depth that we were naturally inclined to turn aside our eyes; here it discharges its impetuous waters by a fall of at least 1000 feet, the spray extends at least a quarter of a mile, and the noise may be plainly heard at the distance of 30 miles—

Jones killed an excellent Buffalo Cow, and by the middle of the after-noon we reached the river banks below the precipices, which, in consequence of the prevalent colour, we called the firey narrows—the distance of this days journey is 29 miles NNE—[46]

---

[45] A short distance above the site of Pathfinder Dam.
[46] Camp was pitched near the location of Alcova, Wyoming.

[November 1812]

Sunday November 1st—Partial showers of sleet and rain fell during the night, and notwithstanding the menacing appearance of the heavens, we crossed the river early and travelled 12 miles, to a stream we called cotton wood Creek on account of the great abundance of those trees which adorn its banks— the bed is sandy, about 40 feet wide, with but little water on its surface, but from appearances a good deal must ooze through its subterraneous passages—In 9 miles from this place, we reached a considerable mountain, through which the river forced its way for 4 miles, when the country opening, it made a larger bend to the north, to the lower end of which we went in two more, and encamped[1] in a beautiful low point of Cotton woods, surrounded with a thick growth of common willow; our days march was 27 miles North east—

The bed of the river is here 150 yards wide, with a very strong current of water—from its northerly course, we now believe it the Cheyenne, tho' for some time we entertained strong hopes of its being rapid river—We saw a great many Buffalo Elk, Ibex & Deer feeding about the base of the mountain—

---

[1] Across from and a mile below Poison Spider Creek.

Monday 2*d.*—We proceeded down 6 miles, when, seeing that the river still bent its course to the north of east, doubts were no longer entertained of our being on the Cheyenne,[2] in consequence of which we held a general consultation, and were unanimously of opinion that by going lower down we might assure ourselves of meeting the Indians from whom the river takes its name; in whose village there being a number of Sioux, their worthy relations on the Missouri would of course be soon advertised of our approach, and lay in ambush for us along the banks of the river in the spring—all were convinced that it was in vain to attempt prosecuting the voyage on foot at this inclement season of the year, thro' such an extensive prairie country, where the procuring of fuel is so extremely precarious; therefore admitting it to be rapid river,[3] and free from all apprehensions of seeing the bad Sioux, all we could gain would be the very agreeable neighborhood of the rascally Puncas, therefore as it was the universal voice that we must undoubtedly winter somewhere on this side of the missouri; I deemed it highly imprudent to go any lower, as it would endanger our safety without the least probable benefit to the expedition; more particularly as our last nights encampment is a situation possessing all the necessary requisites; for here we have wood in abundance, both for building and fuel, and the country round is plentifully stocked with game—

Returning to camp according to agreement, we have determined on passing the winter here, and will leave it on the opening of the navigation, in one or perhaps two Buffalo hide Canoes, till which time we are in strong hopes of living in peace and quiet, without being honoured with the intrusive visits of our savage neighbors—

[2] The headwaters of the Cheyenne were about 135 miles east.
[3] The Niobrara River, about one hundred miles east.

Wednesday 4th—Yesterday five persons went out to hunt, and this evening one of them arrived with the agreeable intelligence of their having killed 32 Buffalo—

Friday 6th—Two feet of Snow fell yesterday, and the weather has since continued so boisterous and severely cold as to freeze the river, which makes a bridge that will greatly diminish the labour of transporting our meat, now collected at the mouth of a small branch,[4] which joins the main stream, one mile above

Saw some Buffalo near camp, but it was too late to attack them—

Sunday 8th—The Buffalo were in the bottom yesterday morning, and by 10 oClock we had killed 15 of them—Commenced building our hut—the weather disagreeably cold—

Tuesday 10th—We were yesterday, and to day, busily employed in transporting our meat to camp and building the hut, all of which business was finished before dusk—our cabin is 8 feet by 18 wide, the fire in the middle, after the Indian fashion, the sides are six feet high, and the whole covered with Buffalo hides, so we have now a tolerable shelter and 47 *black Cattle*—

Thursday 12th—The weather has become so mild as to break up the river—I sent the two Canadians in search of Deer yesterday, for leather to make mogasins &ct, and returned in the evening with 8 Skins of Ibex and black tail'd Deer, and we

[4] Poison Spider Creek. This passage locates the first winter camp.

The Mouth of the Platte

From Catlin's North American Indians

this day procured 20 more, which with a white Bear was the hunt of six persons—

The mountains to the south east are at the distance of 2 miles, the declivity is thickly wooded with Firs and red Cedars, shooting promiscuously out of the crevices of the rocks: in the upper regions, the extensive tracts of pitch pine are occasionally chequered with small patches of quaking Aspen—There are numerous precipices and cut rocky bluffs in different parts of the mountain, which afford a safe retreat to innumerable flocks of Ibex, while the timbered summit and ravines are the residence of many Bear & Black Tail'd Deer—This range is not remarkably high, but its extent to the east, south, & south west is farther than the eye can reach—

[December 1812]

Thursday December 12*th* [10*th*]—Relying with confidence on the snugness of the retreat, which from its isolated situation we supposed sufficiently concealed to elude even the prying investigation of Indian spies, we were astonished, and confounded, at hearing the savage yelp early this morning in the vicinity of our hut—seizing our arms we rushed out, when 23 Arapohays made their appearance, and after the first surprise was over on either side, they advanced in a friendly manner, telling us they were on a war excursion against the Crows, who had some time ago stolen a great many of their Horses, taken some of their women prisoners, and were then on a river six days march to the northward,[1] where they were going in hopes of obtaining revenge; they also related that in passing through the mountain two days ago they heard the report of fire Arms, and on searching, found where two of our people had killed some Deer, which ultimately conducted them to our Cabin; being the sixteenth days march from their village; which is on a large stream[2] from this, nearly due east, but joins the river we are on a great distance below—

[1] The Big Horn or the Yellowstone River.
[2] South Platte River.

Friday 11*th*—The behaviour of the Indians was far more regular and decent than we had any reason to expect from a war party; they threw up two breastworks of Logs, where the whole, excepting the Chief and his deputy, betook themselves to rest tolerably early; these two we permitted to sleep in our hut, and one of us remained awake alternately all night,—

They all ate voraciously, and departed peaceably about 10 A.M. Carrying with them a great proportion of our best meat, in which we willingly acquiesced—They begged a good deal for ammunition, but a peremptory refusal soon convinced them that all demands of that nature were unavailing, and they laughingly relinquished their entreaties—

No sooner were we relieved from the disagreeable company of our guests, than considering the dangerous situation of our residence, with the Crows within two days ride on one side, and the villans[3] who robbed Mr. Miller and the Hunters (on that fork of the Spanish river called big horn[4]) on the other, at the distance of five—and completely satisfied that their good conduct in the present instance was merely to lull our suspicions in ideal security, that they might the better return with a reinforcement and surprise us when least on our guard, we determined to abandon our Chateau of indolence as soon as we can finish the dressing of a sufficiency of leather for Mogasins &ct., that we may be the better able to withstand the severity of the weather—

Our present intention is to extricate ourselves out of the clutches of our rascally neighbours by going a very consider-

[3] Members of the same tribal group as their visitors.

[4] The river known today as the Big Horn flows into the Yellowstone. If the stream referred to is a branch of the Green River, it cannot be identified. And if Stuart meant that his Arapaho guests were traveling to a Crow camp previously described as being distant a six days' ride, there is still no explanation for his reference to the Crows said to be two days away. Possibly this comment refers to information actually given by the Arapahos but not recorded.

able distance down this River, which, from a minute review of the Courses and distance we have come from Henrys Fort and a Map given us by our late visitors, we now believe the rapid River, and if possible make our next cantonement on the banks of the Missouri, but should we not be able to proceed so far, the probability is that we shall at least by this movement be enabled to descend in more durable Canoes than those of Buffalo-skin—

Saturday 12*th*—We this evening finished dressing our leather, and will set out to morrow morg.—

The Indians were kind enough to leave us our faithful quadrupid, not probably for our accommodation, but because he would be more injurious than useful at present, no doubt intending on their return to ease us for ever of any further trouble on his account—

Sunday 13*th*—Left our hut two hours after sun rise, and went 22 miles E by North[5]—The country is extremely barren, only a few Cotton woods to be seen along the river—But many Buffalo rove about in the bottoms—The snow is about 15 inches deep—

Monday 14*th*—We began our march early, and went 27 miles east,[6] over the same kind of country as yesterday, with the snow somewhat deeper than above—The only food we can procure for our horse is Cotton wood bark and Willow tops— saw abundance of game—We are very much fatigued in consequence of the crust not being hard enough to bear us, and our feet are excessively sore, which makes us begin to think

[5] To a spot about a mile east of Evansville, Wyoming.
[6] Eight miles west of the site of Glenrock, Wyoming.

of taking up our quarters in the first eligible situation, and rather than die on the march, fall valiantly on the field of *Mars*.—

Tuesday 15*th*—We travelled 26 miles E by south[7]—and 14 from Camp, we crossed a creek issuing from the mountains on the right, it is nearly 20 yards wide, has a good current of water, and is well timbered with bitter Cotton woods—

the bottoms on the main stream have become extensive and produce Trees sufficiently large for canoes: The River has a gravelly bottom, rapid current, and is 100 yards wide, but the bed is much larger—

Wednesday 16*th*—Going 19 Miles East, we passed two Creeks on the right, near the last of which we found *a large Village of Prairie Dogs, which are nothing more than Ground Squirrel,*—in 8 more S.E. cutting off a very bend, we reached our nights station[8] on the right bank of the river—The range of mountains which began above our late hut, and continued at a short distance parallel with the main stream ever since, has at length subsided into low hills, but about 50 miles to the south, we see another of much greater magnitude—The snow has been upwards of 18 inches deep, but is a good deal reduced by the thaw which began yesterday morning and still continues—

Very few Buffalo were seen during this days march—

Thursday 17*th*—4 miles S.S.E. from Camp we crossed the river, which here ran towards the point of the high mountain, in nearly a south direction—

[7] Opposite the site of Clayton, Wyoming.
[8] Five miles northwest of the location of Douglas, Wyoming.

Went 6 more same course, and 15 E.S.E. to the river, where we encamped[9]—The margin of the stream still continues decorated with considerable bodies of Timber, but the Cotton woods are of a small growth and interspersed with a good many box Alders—

Friday 18*th*—East N.E. 2 miles brought us to a large wooded Fork, entering on the left in a N.N.E. direction, from whose junction the main stream ran 10 due South, partly thro' rocky hills, then 6 east and 1 south, to Camp,[10] where we killed 2 Buffalo, which are much wilder and less numerous than usual—

We at one time to day left the river, in hopes of shortening our route, but found the country so rough that we were compelled to follow the meanders of the stream, and afterwards on the ice, as along its banks—

Saturday 19*th*—To day we followed the meanders of the river 19 miles, the first few through a level tract, and the residue partly on the ice as yesterday—the course were various, but the general one south—Killed an Ibex and encamped[11] at the south of a creek coming from the west, it has a good many Willow and Cotton Wood and among them one ash, the first we have yet seen—

Sunday 20*th*—In our march to day which was 22 miles S.E.[12] we saw a great abundance of Buffalo, Ibex, and Antelopes, and among the timber several Ash and White Oak Trees—

---

[9] About eight miles north-northeast of the present town of Glendo, Wyoming.

[10] Across the river from the site of Cassa, Wyoming.

[11] Opposite the location of Wendover, Wyoming.

[12] About a mile north of the site of Guernsey, Wyoming.

Monday 21*st*—A very small part of this days journey of 23 miles S.E.[13] extricated us from among the narrows we have been in for some time, and the remainder was over a level country—

These Narrows are composed of high rocky hills, with bluffs and precipices on each side of the river, on the declivities of which are numerous Cedars & Pitch Pines, affording an Asylum to great numbers of Ibex & Deer—Since leaving the hills, the snow has almost entirely disappeared, and the weather has every appearance of a mild Autumn

Ash increases fast, and the bottoms are thickly wooded and extensive, with the River running nearly due ease.—

Tuesday 22*d.*—Soon after leaving Camp, the country opened greatly to the eastward, and a well wooded stream, apparently of considerable magnitude, came in from the south west, but whether it is the Arapahay's River, we cannot tell—great numbers of Buffalo & Antelope were seen during this days march; which was 26 miles E.S.E.[14]

Wednesday 23*d.*—Went 18 miles same course,[15] killed two Buffalo and 3 antelope—The bottoms are from 1 to 2 miles wide and thickly covered with cottonwoods some distance back from the margin of the River, which now flows in several channels over a bed of sand—

Thursday 24*th*—The timber gradually diminished all day, and at the end of 27 miles same course,[16] the few trees where

[13] To about the site of Fort Laramie.
[14] To a point near the site of Lingle, Wyoming.
[15] To about three miles below the location of Torrington, Wyoming.
[16] Two miles below where Mitchell, Nebraska, now stands.

we encamped were all we could see—The bottoms became wider, producing grass 8 inches high, on which we saw multitudes of Buffalo feeding this afternoon, and among them a number of wild horses—15 miles above, a fork of large dimensions joined the main river from the south west, and now runs over a sandy bed—in some places half a wile wide.—

Friday 25th—21 Miles same course brought us to camp,[17] in the bare Prairie, but were so fortunate as to find drift wood enough for culinary purposes—

The hills on the south have lately approached the river, they are remarkably rugged and bluffy, possessing a few Cedars—Buffalo very few in number, and mostly Bulls—

Saturday 26th—The extreme coldness of the night made us decamp early, and after travelling 22 miles same course, encamped[18] in a similar situation to that of last night.—Passed a very few scattering trees to day, but not a twig is to be seen to the Eastward—and all kinds of Game, except a few old scabby Bulls, have entirely vanished—The snow has been very deep in this country, is still upwards of 15 inches, tho' none has fallen since we left our hut—

The Bottoms encrease greatly in breadth, indeed the rising ground a few miles off is hardly of sufficient elevation to merit any distinction—

Sunday 27th—The excessive cold made us get up a little before dawn, when taking into consideration that having last evening seen at least 50 miles to the eastward, without any

[17] Near the location of Minatare, Nebraska.
[18] About the site of Bayard, Nebraska.

indications to timber, and should there be some little drift-wood about the banks of the river, the depth of snow is too great to admit of our finding it: deprecating therefore the wretchedness of our situation should we be overtaken in these boundless plains by a snow storm, particularly, as we have reason to expect it daily, and the country before us such an inhospitable waste as to be deserted even by every kind of Quadrupid—we soon concluded that our best plan was to return up the river, to where we should find Buffalo, for our *support* and timber for Canoes;

The bed of the river is here 1½ mile wide, composed of quicksand; cut into innumerable Channels with very low banks and destitute of even a single twig—This being so different from the character we ever heard of the rapid river; our having southed so much of late, and its appearance coinciding exactly with that of the great River Platte, we have strong inducements to believe, that we are on the main branch of the last mentioned stream—We accordingly retraced our steps and took up our nights station, 4 miles above our camp of the 25th Inst.—[19]

Monday 28*th*—Passed our encampment of 24th Inst., about 6 miles,[20] and stopped early, have killed 3 Buffalo

The wind blew strong from the west all day, and we find it intensely cold—

Tuesday 29*th*—This morning we saw several herds of Buffalo scattered all over the prairie—crossed the main river a little above the wooded fork,[21] the ice was entirely gone, but fortunately the water was not in any of the channels more

[19] About four miles above the site of Minatare.
[20] Therefore about four miles above the location of Mitchell.
[21] Horse Creek.

than knee deep—The fork is about 50 yards wide, up which we proceeded 3 miles in hopes of finding an eligible situation, as we conceived this an excellent spot for Game, but on a close examination, found the trees too small for Canoes—

Wednesday 30*th*—Leaving Camp after breakfast, we went up the main stream 12 miles, to opposite the first large body of woods, where we killed four Buffalo, and Leclaire, who had crossed the river below in quest of Canoe trees, came to us with the agreeable tidings of his having found three—We brought in the meat and encamped[22] among some scattering timber near the bank—

Thursday 31*st*—At an early hour, we crossed the river, which was running thick with ice, and took up our residence close to the bank, and by the middle of the day we had a shelter made and our meat scaffolded—Began building our hut, one side of which we raised before dusk.—

[22] Across from and a little below the site of Torrington, Wyoming.

[January 1813]

Friday January 1st 1813—Was solely devoted to the gratification of our appetites: all work was suspended for the day, and we destroyed an immoderate quantity of Buffalo Tongues, Puddings, and the choicest of the meat—Our stock of Virginia weed being totally exhausted, Mr. McClellan's Tobacco Pouch was cut up and smoked as a substitute, in commemoration of the new year.—

Saturday Jan 9th—Our hut, tho' incomplete, we took possession of on the 2d. inst., had it finished on the 6th., and killed 17 Buffalo the following day: This day we felled our Canoe Trees, and found them all hollow, but chose the two best, and began working them—

[March 1813]

Sunday March 7th—The river having been open for several days, and the weather promising a continuation of the thaw, we dragged our Canoes to the bank, and prepared them for our reception tomorrow morning—One wild goose made her appearance this afternoon and was killed for dinner—

Monday 8th—Breakfasting at an early hour we embarked, but in descending a few hundred yards, found the water so low that Mr. McClellan and myself went by land, hoping thereby that the Canadians would be able to proceed—The other Canoe being small went on tolerably, but it was with considerable labour in wading and dragging that ours was got down 8 miles by the middle of the afternoon, when finding an Indian *Pen* sufficient to screen us from the severity of the weather, we stopped in it,[1] determined to wait the rise of the water

Monday 15th—I sent back to the hut for our horse yesterday, and this morning, the river having risen 5 or 6 inches, we embarked a small part of our baggage (and four of us) in the Canoes, while the residue was carried by our good old

[1] About a mile west of the present Wyoming–Nebraska state line.

Rozinante, we went on pretty well to the fork, but immediately below, the river became much wider and so shallow that it was with great exertion we reached another Pen, on the left bank, 7 miles below our last station, where we found our people who had gone by land; here we took up our lodgings,[2] pretty much tired of this new mode of inland navigation, *and resolved on taking our land tacks on board again* unless the river rises soon to such a height as will assure us of getting on to a certainty by the common mode of paddling—

Saturday 20*th*—It snowed with but little intermission during the 16th & 17th inst., and excepting a little thaw towards the 18th & 19th, the weather has of late been worse than any we experienced throughout the winter, in consequence of which, and being very doubtful whether we can in any reasonable time proceed by water, it was agreed that we should try it once more on foot, and we accordingly continued down the left bank to our encampment of 27th December, where we halted for the night—[3]

Sunday 21*st.*—We travelled till late in the afternoon, and stopped a mile above our camp of 26th Dec.[4]—Killed a very fat goose, which, as well as Buffalo, have been abundant all along—

Monday 22*d*—We encamped this evening,[5] 23 miles lower than we have yet been on this river—

Nothing but a boundless plain, plentifully stocked with animals, appears before us, and the river, running East South east, so shallow that we are now convinced of the impossibility of getting along in Canoes, for its bed for the most part

[2] South of the site of Morrill, Nebraska.
[3] About four miles above present-day Minatare.
[4] About one mile above the site of Bayard.
[5] Five or six miles below where Northport, Nebraska, now stands.

is upwards of a mile wide, and the sand bars so numerous and flat that it would require more water than we have any right to expect to have made it fit for our purposes—

Tuesday 23*d*.—About midnight the wind, which has been for some time from the East, veered to the north, blew with violence, and was withal so cold that our bed-Cloths appeared as if converted into seives, we were in the bare prairie, and our fuel what little dry Buffalo dung we could collect—We set out soon after daylight, and stopped at the end of 26 miles same course[6]

The hills on the opposite side of the river approached much nearer than usual this afternoon, & possess some timber, but whether Pine or Cedar, or both, we cannot tell—on our side, there is not a twig to be seen, and the rising grounds seldom come within less than 3 miles of the river—

Wednesday 24*th*—This days march was 29 miles long, over a similar tract to that passed for a number of days, with the agreeable variation of finding half a dozen withered Cotton woods to encamp at,[7]

The hills on the south are much higher than on our side and keep close to the river, which making the low prairie in general very narrow, the Buffalo have but an indifferent range, and apparently prefer the north side, where the plain is for the most part a mile wide, with abundance of excellent grass for their support—

Thirteen miles back, a creek with a very sandy bed and a good many trees on its banks joined the main stream from the south, but was not of any depth of water—The weather continues extremely cold, with the wind from the east—

[6] About three miles above the site of Lisco, Nebraska.
[7] About three miles below present-day Oshkosh, Nebraska.

Thursday 25*th*—We remained in the same camp all day, Mr. Miller's feet being so much blistered as to render him totally unfit to travel; besides the wind from the eastward was too strong and piercingly cold to encourage our pressing forward, particularly as every one was very willing to rest—Some Bulls coming near camp, we put 3 of them to the *sword,* and with their hides made a comfortable shelter—

Friday 26*th*—Our journey to day was 27 miles same course and kind of country,[8]—13 miles from last nights camp, we crossed a creek 30 yards wide, coming about N.N.W. and issuing from among sandy hills; there were a few trees on its banks, and from the appearance of the water it must run thro' an excellent soil somewhat farther up—

3 miles lower, another branch joined the main stream from the south; it is thickly wooded a short distance from its mouth, but with what kinds we could not well distinguish—

For a considerable way above, but more particularly below its junction, the river bluffs are very near, and sometimes constitute its banks; they are principally composed of a blue lime stone, and possess many Cedars, on which account we call the last mentioned branch *Cedar Creek.*—

Saw 65 wild horses, and for the last 3 day's march, the country is (I may say) literally covered with buffalo—

Saturday 27*th*—Some distance above and below last nights station is an extensive swamp, the resort of innumerable numbers of Geese, Brants, a few Swans, and an endless variety of Ducks; during the latter part of this days march, we found several similar places, all well stocked with wild fowl—The country on our side is little else than sand, but where the bot-

[8] Six miles above the site of Lemoyne, Nebraska.

toms have the least claim to goodness of soil, they produce a considerable growth of straw, being the first we have seen since leaving the Columbia bottoms.—Passed two creeks issuing from the sandy bluffs to the N.E. and encamped opposite an Island, on which I killed 3 swans and a Goose with one shot, the distance across the river was 170 yards—29 miles East by South was the length of this days march[9]—In walking among the straw in the neighborhood of our camp, we raised 5 Pheasants, or as they are called in this country, Prairie Hens —this induces us to believe the Missouri bottoms not far distant, as these creatures have never been known to progress any great distance into the interior—[10]

Sunday 28*th*—Today we went 27 miles due east,[11] the greater part thro' low wet grounds, and the remainder over barren sand—The hills on the south have very much diminished in size, and sand now appears to be the principal part of their composition; on our side they are, with the exception of a few spots, wholly of that material, but the bottoms are again of a superior quality, and produce grass in abundance for the multitudes of Buffalo roving thereon—

The country is still without timber, and as far as we can see is almost destitute of even a hill; the river is generally from three quarters to a mile wide, but for the most part too shallow to float even an empty Canoe—

Monday 29*th*—Our course was 12 miles E by North, then passing over a range of sand hills, whose base was washed by the river, we in 9 more east crossed a stream 100 yards wide, running over a bed of quick sand and about waist deep—

[9] About a mile below the site of Kingsley Dam.
[10] The Missouri River was about 280 miles away.
[11] Across the river from the location of Sarben, Nebraska.

Sawyers and Planters in the Missouri

Here the hills on both side, especially those on the south, receded to a greater distance than has been the case since we left the head waters of the river, and by the time we reached camp[12] at the end of 10 miles more, same course, they were at least 27 miles apart—on collecting fuel among the drift wood, we found a number of pieces cut by an axe, close to the ground, but whether they are chopped in this manner on account of their being too wet or too hard frozen to be extracted by the application of the hands along, we cannot tell, so are at a loss to say at what season, or who the people were that left these vestiges—On the other side, there is every appearance of a large stream[13] having broke thro' the hills, but we have not yet seen the entrance; however it possesses a few trees and Buffalo without number.—Before us the country somewhat resembles the Ocean, with a promentory projecting from the north, for on the South the View is bounded by the horizon alone—There is yet no timber, but a small growth of Willows all along the main shore and on almost every island, which gives us great hopes of finding at no very great distant day trees of such size, and number, as will put an end to the dreary sameness of the prairie wastes— The weather has at length become very mild, and to wards noon it is too hot to be agreeable, particularly to a poor Devil with a heavy budget on his back—

Tuesday 30*th*—8 Miles east brought us to an Indian encampment of considerable magnitude, and in the course of the day we passed two others, which from all appearance were occupied last fall by people who seem to have valued the animals they killed, for we found numerous marks of their having stretched skins; all the Buffalo skulls had the brains taken

[12] About eight miles above the site of North Platte, Nebraska.
[13] South Platte River.

out, the dung lying in heaps, contrary to the custom of Wolves, convinced us that even the paunches had been preserved, and at the last Camp we found a number of the *Cobs of Indian Corn,* from all of which we suppose these signs were made by the Panees or Ottos, more particularly as in the afternoon we reached an Island with large timber on its borders, which answering to the description of one we have heard of as being some distance above the Loup Fork of the Platte, we are willing to believe ourselves there—One mile above the Island, the large stream from the south[14] joined the main river, but as we could not get opposite its entrance on account of swamps, I have only the account of our people who when hunting saw it from the hills, and say that it is at least as large as the one we descended.—The hills on the south come close to the river immediately below its mouth, and from thence downwards, as far as the eye can carry, we see large bodies of timber all along their base, which seem to keep close in the vicinity of the other Channel of the river, while on one side they are about 3 miles distant—

We travelled 26 miles E by South, when being opposite the first woods on the Island we encamped,[15] having come 33 miles thro' bottoms of rich lands producing straw six feet high, and four miles above our present station, watered by a Creek 20 Yards wide, about knee deep, its banks well lined with willow, and possessing numerous Beaver—Prickly pears, Antelopes, and wild horses, have completely disappeared within the last 3 days, but our dearly beloved friends the Buffalo still remain to comfort our solitary wanderings, and five Fallow Deer ran across our path some distance above—.

[14] This was the South Platte; Stuart was now at Brady Island.
[15] About seven miles above the site of Gothenburg, Nebraska.

[April 1813]

Thursday April 1st—Having killed 2 Buffalo, and both ourselves and horse being a good deal inclined to rest, we did not leave Camp yesterday—We set out at an early hour this morning, and travelled 25 miles East, 6 east by south, & 3 S.E. to a low point, where we encamped[1] without any other fuel than small dry Willows and Buffalo dung, neither of which were very abundant—Our route was thro' the bare prairie all day, but following the Indian trace, we traversed only one swamp, tho' from the number of Wild fowl there must have been many in the neighborhood—

The Island has as yet abounded with timber, but not a single tree decorates the main shore—

The southern hills have become much higher, and very steep, with many wooded ravines, but on our side they still retain their former insignificance—We had a great deal of both Thunder and Lightning before sun set, which made us put up our little Tent, but a small shower only fell during the night—In the evening we saw a few Fallow Deer & 17 Elk—

Friday 2d.—A short distance below camp, we passed the end of the Island, so that if this is the *grand Isle* of the River

---

[1] Three miles west of the location of Willow Island.

Platte, instead of its being 90 miles long and 30 broad, it does not exceed 32 in length and 10 in width—in other respects, it agrees with our information, for the banks are well lined with timber, as is also the southern main shore, but ours is still woefully deficient in that article—We followed the trail 15 miles E.S.E. and 12 S.E. by E, when the atmosphere indicating bad weather inclined us to stop for the night[2] in a large thicket of willow, but before we could erect our shelter, it began to rain heavily and continued so till midnight—

The hills on this side became gradually lower till within the last 6 miles, when they disappeared entirely and a range of greater elevation, about 12 miles off, have assumed their place—

Saturday 3d.—Our days march was 25 miles S E. by East, and 1 East along the Indian path,[3] which suddenly vanished a short distance back, so we are, as formerly obliged to take the river for our guide—there was no timber of any consequence on either side yesterday or to day, what little we see are small Cottonwoods, which are wholly on the numerous Islands with which the river abounds, its bed is upwards of 2 miles wide, and of course very shallow—Early this forenoon we discovered about 10 miles to our left a few scattering trees, which gradually increased in number till opposite our encampment, when they were augmented to a considerable stripe of woods, about 6 miles off, with the range of hills we first saw yesterday running parallel in the vicinity—That some water course is near us on the North, we have not the least doubt, but knowing of no other but the Loup Fork, and thinking ourselves not so far advanced, we are at a loss what to make of it, we nevertheless hope for the best, and shall not be sorry

[2] Seven miles above the site of Lexington, Nebraska.
[3] Three miles southeast of the same location.

to find it what we dare hardly expect—saw four Animals on the other side of the river, which we believe to be Buffalo— but on ours we have not seen any for the last two days, and very few old vestiges—

Sunday 4th—After travelling 8 miles E.S.E. we crossed the river, where it was divided into 10 Channels, with a bed of such quick sand that it was difficult for our horse to get over, tho' the water was in no place more than two feet deep,

Soon after making the southern bank, we found the Indian path, which following 9 miles, we passed a Creek 20 yards wide, with some willows, and where it issued from the hills about 4 miles above, a few trees of the Pine species— several other little guts ran across our way, but we supposed them the drains of swamps—The hills on this side have dwindled almost to nothing, and those of the other, which are beyond the stripe of wood we saw yesterday and continued to see all this day, have also lost some of their height, but the fork has not as yet added its waters to the main stream— About a mile back, we found a straw hut in an old Indian encampment inhabited by 3 squaws, who appeared very much terrified on our approach, but after a little time gave us to understand they were Panees, but altho' we spoke to them in the language of their neighbours the Ottos and gave them some dried meat, with other demonstrations of our friendship, yet they continued much agitated, and told us nothing we could comprehend, except that there were white people in the country, at no great distance—The total of this days journey was 11 miles S.E. by E. 15 E.S.E. & 6 E. by South—[4]

[4] Four miles directly south from the site of the town of Elm Creek, Nebraska.

Monday 5th—We came 29 miles E. by South,[5] along the Indian trace, which on leaving camp consisted of 3 paths, but from the middle of the day till we stopped, they increased to ten, all running parallel

The water course[6] we saw the wood on for two days past joined the main stream 10 miles back, but it is impossible for us to say how large or what it is: below its junction, by a considerable body of large timber, which runs down as far as we can see, and the hills of that side, about the same place, appear to have either turned off abruptly to the left, or resumed their former character and become part of the plain—Killed 2 Geese and two swans, and in the craws of the latter found several of the identical root dug by the Natives of the Columbia below the Falls of that river, and Called by them Wapatoes—

Tuesday 6th—26 miles East was the length of this days *walk*[7]—The body of timber has encreased greatly, and extends too far to the north for the eye to distinguish its width, we are nevertheless obliged to wade a narrow channel to procure fuel, as well as food for our horse; the grass on the main having been totally consumed by fire, and all the wood is on an Island, which from every appearance must be the Grand Isle; if so we are now about 140 miles from the mouth of the Platte—[8]

There are no hills to be seen on the other side, and for the last two day's march those on this side have been extremely low, and never come within 4 or 5 miles of the river—The timber now consists of Cotton wood, Elm, Box Alder, Ash, and white willow, with an almost impenetrable under growth

[5] To the location of Newark, Nebraska.

[6] Possibly a channel on the north side of the Platte.

[7] To a spot five miles east of the site of Denman, Nebraska.

[8] Here Stuart's surmise is correct. The distance by river between this point and the Missouri is about 175 miles.

of Arrow wood, common & red willow, &ct. notwithstanding all this, but few of the furr'd race are induced to inhabit the banks—Since leaving the Columbian plains, we have found few or no esculent roots untill this afternoon, when we fell in with a large field of the root called by the Ottos "Toe" & by the Canadians "Pomme de Terre," they are but seldom of larger dimensions than a hens egg, with a rough warty brown skin, are never more than 6 inches deep in the earth, and when boiled, resemble very much in taste the *sweet potato*—saw several Fallow Deer, and of late Kurlews and old field Larks are the only birds, except water Fowl, that we see—

Wednesday 7th—Soon after leaving Camp it began to rain very hard, which continued partially all day—at the end of 23 miles East, finding good feed for our pony, who is extremely weak and jaded, we stopped on a small Island for the night[9]—A number of little Islands are scattered promiscuously along the Channel, they possess some Beaver and a good deal of small wood, while that on the big one is very large and of too great an extent for the eye to measure—on our side, there is seldom a twig, but we have again come to the unburnt prairie—during the first part of this days march the hills were very near the river, but they soon receded, and are now about the same distance as for some days back—André Vallée killed a Fallow Deer, which is the first we have been able to lay our claws on; it is very poor, but as our stock of dried meat (which we have been keeping in reserve) is getting very low, we are glad of any addition—

Thursday 8th—9 Miles E.N.E. 9 N E by East and 11 N.E. brought us to our nights lodging,[10] in a more extensively

[9] Seven miles directly south of the location of Alda, Nebraska.
[10] About five miles down the river from the site of Phillips, Nebraska.

wooded bottom than we have met with since we have left our
winter quarters—

The hills came close to the river in the early part of the
day, and have since continued in the vicinity; they are low,
but much broken, and possess good soil, producing a short
kind of grass, which our horse is very fond of, and is apparently in his estimation nearly equal to rushes, now found in
great plenty on the Islands—The grand Isle terminated two
miles back is according to our judgment 72 miles long, and if
we may calculate, in the same ratio its width is about 24—It
has throughout possessed great bodies of timber, affording
shelter and sustenance to a good many Elk, Deer, and a few
Beaver—ever since we lost sight of the Buffalo, their dung
and other sign of last winter, as also Indian encampments of
same time, have been seen every where, from which we are
confident a number of the Panee nation have wintered on the
Platte, and from the snow being yet visible on the last hills we
saw to the North, that season must have been very severe, else
the Buffalo would not have come so low, which from all we
can now discover is very uncommon—These Indians travelled
towards the south early in the spring, when those animals no
doubt left the woods, so the three women we found in one of
their Camps must have been sick, and there abandoned to their
fate by their savage relations—Every appearance of savage
and Buffalo is at an end, all the freshest roads crossed the big
Island, which we suppose the route to their present Towns
on the Loup fork, so we have now to rely on an indistinct
path, formerly very extensive, but not travelled in some years,
which in the end we hope will lead us to the old Panee Village near the mouth of the above Fork—The river is about
the same breadth as formerly, much broken by innumerable
Islands, in which the most of the timber generally is—Jones
killed a Deer close to Camp—

Friday 9*th*—Our journey to day was 6 miles E.N.E. 17 E by N. and 4 N.W by E. when a heavy gust of rain obliged us to encamp on an Island[11]—The hills on this side continue as yesterday, but nothing can be seen on the other but a smooth burnt prairie

The Indian path has become scarcely discernible, and in many places not a vestige remains; however, as the uplands are close to the river, we find it good walking, as the grass on them is for the most part very short, a great difference from the bottoms where it is generally 5 Feet high—

Saturday 10*th*—The road was still visible, and along it we travelled 12 miles E.N.E. 9 E. by N. & 13 east, to our nights station,[12] on an Island as usual—The opposite shore seems equally destitute of timber with this, and the hills of either side (if I may be allowed a Bull) are low prairie: indeed it is extraordinary, tho' no less true, that while the main land possesses but few trees, and often not even a willow, yet there is scarcely an Island of however diminutive dimensions but is wholly covered with wood.—

It is hardly possible to guess at the width of the river, as we but seldom see the whole at once on account of the numerous islands which are scattered from shore to shore, but so far as we can judge, it is about 2 to 3 miles, which has been the case for the last three or four days—We saw a number of Fallow Deer (the only kind to be seen), one of whom Jones took the life of—The weather is occasionally so hot as to be truly disagreeable—

Sunday 11*th*—About 8 miles from Camp an Indian of the Otto Nation overtook us, with whom I sent back two of our

[11] Four miles southeast of the location of Clarks, Nebraska.
[12] Four miles southwest of the site of Columbus, Nebraska.

people to their camp, for the purpose of getting news and finding out exactly where we are—7 miles farther on the Loup fork entered from the North, it is upwards of 200 yards wide, a clear rapid stream, with about 5 feet water, to follow the Channel to the Padeau Fork, a distance of 99 miles—45 miles from the mouth is Beaver Creek, 10 yards wide—30 farther up is willow river 45 yards broad—12 more takes you to Corn field Creek 20 yards between the banks, where now stands the Grand Panee Village, of about 900 warriors, under the sach-emship of Kee-taw-rou, or long hair—one league farther on the Panee Mahaa Village (of 650 fighting men) stands on the margin of a branch, in size the same as that of the Village below; Ash-ay-koy-pay-row, or the Chief's knife, is their head —9 miles higher the Padeau fork 80 yards wide joins the main stream—and 18 more takes you to that of Pomme de Terre, equal in size with the last, from whence it is at least 450 miles, by the meanders of the river, to its source, in several Lakes of considerable extent, situated in the beautiful high plain.—

The main stream above the mouth of Pomme de Terre is apparently but little diminished in size, and the timber which every where below decorates its borders gradually be-comes less plenty, and at its final separation into small branches, wood is to be found only in patches—

All the tributary streams enumerated above join the main river from the south, they are well wooded, and give refuge to a good many of the furr'd race; besides their wooded re-cesses give shelter to innumerable Deer and Elk, with a few Bear—The Panee Makaas, or Loups, for the most part rove from their Town to the extremities of the Fork which bears their name, but the big village, crossing the Loup Fork and intervening plain, pass the river Platte, and following it to nearly the end of the timbered tract, below ringing water river, where they generally make their Buffalo hunt—sometimes they even penetrate to the frontier Villages of New Mexico, but we cannot say that their range passes the northern forks of the above stream—

These Indians come to their Towns early in april, plant their Corn, Pumpkins, and Beans towards the end of may, stay untill they are a certain height, when leaving it to the benign care of the all seeing providence, and return to the plains to pursue the hump backed race—In August they revisit their Village, and after gathering in the harvest, depositing it safely and securely in excavations made for the purpose in the earth, they once more leave their homes for their favorite pursuit of the Buffalo, at which they employ themselves until the following april—

The Grand Panees make annually about 150 packs of Buffalo robes and 20 of Beaver, and the Loups 100 of the former and 12 of the latter, this may be considered as the average, but in a good year they will have as many more—We came on 6 miles to where the Grand Panee Village stood, on an elevated bank of the Platte, about 4 years ago—and 17 more brought us to Camp, at a large point of Woods, where we killed a Turky, the first we have seen—The total distance of to days march was 38 miles in nearly a due east direction—[13]

Monday 12*th*—Early in the morning Mr. Crooks & Vallée overtook us—They had walked till long after dark, but the night being too dark to discover us, they slept at a little distance from our Camp—They went 6 miles back with the Indian, where they found two families of Ottos, who informed them that Mr. François Doruin was the trader at their village; and that for a year past, the Americans and English were at war—They said the distance to their Town was two days

[13] Five miles directly south of the site of Schuyler, Nebraska.

march—17 miles from Camp we passed a Creek, where a village of Panees formerly lived—Next we followed the road along the foot of the hills for 8 more, when ascending the ridge it began to rain heavily, which compelled us to make for a point of Wood on the Platte, where we stopped for the night,[14] having come in all 31 miles E.S.E.—

Tuesday 13*th*—4 miles nearly south brought us to the trace which passed in the vicinity of a branch of the saline river, over a high plain 23 miles, then ascending a ridge of considerable elevation, we in 6 more reached the Otto Village,[15] standing about 400 yards from the right bank of the Platte— The river is three quarters of a mile wide, with some Islands, which as well as the opposite shore are thickly covered with Cottonwoods, Ash, Oak, Hickory, &ct.—

The day was extremely cold for the season, and in the afternoon several showers of sleet and hail fell—

Here we found Mr. F. Doruin and Mr. Roi, who after a voyage of 6 weeks from St. Louis reached this place three days ago—On the Missouri, the winter was severe, beyond any seen in this Country for the last 20 years, the snow was 4½ feet deep, and all out of door work could not be accomplished without the assistance of snow shoes—.

The disagreeable news of a war between America & Great Britain was here confirmed, but in such a confused manner was it related that we could comprehend but little—We gave Mr. Doruin our Horse, who in return is to get us a skin Canoe and provisions sufficient to take us to Fort Osage, where, if we find no conveyance to St. Louis, we can no doubt get the proper means of constructing a Canoe, which the People here are totally destitute of—

[14] About two miles east of the location of Morse Bluff, Nebraska.
[15] Two miles southeast of the site of Yutan, Nebraska.

Wednesday 14*th*—Some snow fell in the course of the night, and so cold was the day that nothing could be done towards making our Canoe other than putting the hides in the river to soak—

The Ottos and Missouris are of equal force, & jointly can bring 300 fighting men into the field,—they had resided together for a number of years, and by marriage have become so intermixed that we may at this day justly call them the same people, more particularly as their habits, manners, customs, and pursuits are exactly the same—Many lodges are about to be constructed, but the Village consists at present of only 30, containing from two to four families each—all are much of a size and built in the following manner, being every way the same as those of the Panee's, except that the latter are much larger—

From a pole stuck in that spot of ground intended for the centre of the fabric, a cord upwards of 40 feet long is extended, which, carrying round the extremity, is marked every 10 feet by the incursion of a small stick in the earth, making an area of at least 100 feet in circumference—Forked poles 8 feet high and 4 inches in diameter are next put firmly in the ground, taking place of the pegs & making the extreme of the circle—across these are laid straight pieces of wood, of the same size, and others considerably smaller, having one end in the earth, are leaned against the last—Six large strong forks are then set up half way between the extremes, and circled, 12 feet high, on which powerful beams are placed as before, serving as a support to 120 poles running from the first elevation to the middle, where a hole 2 feet wide is left to emit the smoke—Willows are laid across the last poles every where, with a good covering of straw firmly attached thereto, and one foot of earth being beat down hard over all completes the mansion, excepting the entrance, from which runs out an erection of similar materials, 7 feet high, 6 wide,

and 15 long—The door is generally an Elk or Buffalo hide—
The floor is 18 inches lower than the earth outside, and for
the fire place the ground in the centre of the building is scraped
away, so as to make it the lowest place in the lodge, and from
near it, a pole surpassing in height any put in the roof is put
out at the chimney, where are suspended their medecine bags
and war Budgets, carefully concealed in innumerable wrap-
pers, which effectually protects them from the influence of
the weather—

Friday 16*th*—Our Canoe was finished last evening and consists of five Elk & Buffalo hides, sewed together with strong
sinews, drawn over and made fast to a frame composed of
poles and Willows 20 feet long, 4 wide, and 18 inches deep,
making a vessel somewhat shaped like a Boat, very steady, and
by the aid of a little mud on the seams, remarkably tight—in
this we embarked at an early hour and drifted 10 miles, when
the wind began making Oars an absolute necessary part of our
equipment, and not to be procured at the Indian Village,—2
miles back we passed the Elk horn River, coming from the
North, the water is exceedingly black, the current strong, its
banks well lined with cotton woods and Willows, the resort
of many Beaver & otter—

Sunday 18*th*—We completed our set of Oars yesterday morning, but the wind continued too high to try them.

4 miles from the camp we passed the saline, a considerable stream coming from the south, and in 31 more reached
the Missouri—The Platte, from the Otto village to its mouth,
keeps about its former course, and is in every respect much
the same as we found it from ringing water,[16] with the excep-

16 Plum Creek.

tion of the hills possessing a beautiful growth of oak, and the other timber is not as formerly confined to the Islands alone—

Thursday 22*d.*—On the 19th we came 65 miles, and passed a creek called weeping water[17]—the next day, on account of bad weather, we travelled only 27,[18] and saw the little me-makaa and Nish-na-la-ta-nay rivers—yesterday brought us to the black snake hills,[19] 63 from last nights Camp, having seen today big and little Taw-go-you, woolf Creek, and Now-doway River, but this days march was only 20 miles long,[20] as we were compelled by a strong head wind to put a shore by 10 oClock, and we passed the remainder of the day making a new frame for our Canoe, as the old one had become unfit for the purpose—I sent out two hunters, who soon returned with two Deer and 4 Turkys—

Saturday 24*th*—Yesterday we started at an early hour, and at the end of 68 miles encamped at a Wintering place of last season,[21] where we found two Old wooden Canoes, and took possession of the largest—Having travelled 55 miles, we in the afternoon arrived at Fort Osage,[22] where we got satisfactory information of the melancholy truth of war having been waged since June last between the United States and Great Britain—

The Fortification was built in the fall of 1808, by a Company of regulars under the Command of Capt. Climson,

[17] Camp was about seven miles west of the site of Hamburg, Iowa.

[18] To a point about three miles west of the location of Watson, Missouri.

[19] About five miles southwest of the present city of St. Joseph, Missouri.

[20] To a portion of the river lying ten miles north-northeast of the site of Atchison, Kansas.

[21] On the ground now occupied by the city of Leavenworth, Kansas.

[22] Five miles southwest of the site of Orrick, Missouri.

and has been the means of reducing the turbulent Kanzes to a proper sense of the true relation in which Indians stand with their civilized neighbours—there is a united states Factory here for all Tribes who may choose to come for the purpose of trade, but more particularly for the Osages, who resided in the environs some time ago, but at present have their villages on the Osage River—

In this days journey we passed the little river Platte, Blue water, the Cabin de Paille,[23] and the Kanzes River, called after the Indians of that name, who live on it about 80 leagues from the mouth—a band of Panees also live on a fork of it; they are upwards of 600 in number, occupied some years ago the same town with the Grand Panees on the Platte, and on account of their revolt from the others have since been known by the name of Republicans, which title is also been given to that branch of the Kanzes River where their village stands—

Monday 26th—In consequence of bad weather we remained all yesterday at Fort Osage, and were very hospitably entertained by Lieut. Brownson (who commands in the absence of Major Climson) he furnished us very generously with a sufficiency of Pork, Flour, &ct. to carry us to St. Louis—This days journey was 70 miles,[24] in the course of which we passed Eber's & Fiery Prairies Creeks and Tabeau's River, as also a place called the Old little Osage Village, where the Tribe of that name resided a great many years ago—

Friday 30th—Setting out early on the 27th, we passed grand Charaton and Le mine River, a distance of 75 miles[25]—during

---

[23] Little Blue River.
[24] About five miles below the mouth of the Grand River.
[25] To about the site of Boonville, Missouri.

Item from the *Missouri Gazette*
St. Louis, Saturday, May 8, 1813

the following day we saw the entrance of Big and Little Bonne Femme, Big & Little Manitoes, Bear split Rock, Moreau & Cedar Creeks, also the Osage River[26]—68 miles   yesterday we came to the Cave in Rock, a distance of 78 miles[27]—leaving behind us the two muddy creeks,[28] those Called Loutre Charette, Shepherds[29] & Woods,[30] with that fine stream the Gasconude—

Immediately on entering the Missouri at the mouth of the River Platte, we found both the main land and Islands thickly covered with Timber of but few kind, but as we progressed the variety became greater, till at its junction with the Mississippi we could enumerate Cotton-wood, Sycamore, Ash—Hackberry—Walnut—Hickory—Box Alder—Mulberry—Elm—and Oak besides the smaller growths of Dog wood & Papa,[31] with an end less variety of under brush— Game is not in the greatest abundance in the vicinity of the Platte, but from a little distance below to near the mouth of the Missouri, Elk, Deer, Black Bear—Racoons—wild cats, and Turkeys are to be found in great plenty on the land, while the rivers furnish a good many Beaver & Otter, with a variety of excellent Fish—

The soil is wonderfully fertile, but its fertility is not equal throughout the Country, principally owing to the many rugged hills with which it is interspersed, these altho' not susceptible of any agricultural improvement, still afford excellent pasture—

2d.[32] The Ottos and Missouris on the Platte make an-

[26] About five miles below the mouth of the Osage River.

[27] About twelve miles north of the location of Eureka, Missouri.

[28] Auxvasse and Little Auxvasse creeks.

[29] Berger Creek.

[30] St. John's Creek.

[31] Papaw.

[32] This figure, like the one on the next page, may indicate some plan of organization.

nually about 250 packs of skins, of which it is common to find 40 of Beaver—The Republican Panees generally bring out the same quantity and kinds as their relations, the big Village on the Platte—In the village of 350 Kanzes is to be found about 200 packs, among which are from 20 to 30 of Beaver—The Osages are said to be upwards of 1500 Warriors, and can produce on an average 500 packs, but the quantity of Beaver is not so great in proportion as at the Ottos and Missouris—

1st. The missouri from where we struck it to its entrance is upwards of 600 miles, and from ¼ to a mile wide—a rapid Current—the water intolerably muddy, and every bend of it is filled with sawyers and planters,[33] occasioned by the falling in of the banks, which carrying the trees along with them, the roots become immoveably fixed in the bed of the river and form an object of considerable risk to persons unacquainted with such a navigation.—

The Christian settlements extend 198 miles up the Missouri, made principally by emigrants from Kentucky, who (if it had not been for the present war) would have advanced much farther, but for the present content themselves within the Fortifications they have constructed on account of the Indians; and raise a bare sufficiency for the sustenance of their families.—

This day after descending 35 miles, we a little before sun set reached the Town of St. Louis, all in the most perfect health, after a voyage of ten months from Astoria, during which time we underwent many dangers, hardships, & fatigues, in short, I may say, all the privations human nature is capable of.

The distance from St. Louis to N. York	1345 miles
add distance from Astoria to St Louis	3768
Total Distance from Astoria to N. York	5113 miles

[33] Tree trunks. Sawyers bob up and down, while planters lie motionless.

Appendix I

The Manuscript of the
"Travelling Memoranda"

On May 13, 1930, a worn ledger book was placed on sale by the American Art Association–Anderson Galleries, Incorporated, reappearing after almost one hundred years. Purchased by William Robertson Coe for his collection of Western Americana, it remained in his possession until 1948, when he bequeathed the collection to the Yale University Library.

According to the catalogue of the sale the "Travelling Memoranda" "was found in a cupboard at Sunnyside by E. M. Grinnell, grandnephew of Washington Irving, and had remained in possession of the family till now."[1] This brief note constitutes the only evidence regarding the location of the manuscript between the years 1836 and 1930 and, scant though it is, must be relied upon until further indications appear. Fortunately there is no reason to doubt the statement. Irving undoubtedly had possession of the manuscript during or before 1836, and there is no indication of its having appeared between then and the time of its sale.

The history of the "Travelling Memoranda" prior to 1836 is equally obscure. The only indication of its whereabouts is found in the *Nouvelles Annales*.[2] Here the "Travelling

[1] Catalogue of the American Art Association–Anderson Galleries, Sale No. 3850, May 12 and 13, 1930, p. 31.

[2] *Nouvelles Annales des Voyages, de la Geographie et de l'Histoire*, Vols. X and XII, April and October, 1821.

Memoranda" is to be found in a French translation about 8,000 words shorter than the original.[3] Philip Ashton Rollins has fairly described the quality of the translation in the following words: "the French text in *Nouvelles Annales,* when compared with the English text in the travelling memoranda [*sic*] is shown to have ineptly converted various of Stuart's creeks and hills into rivers and mountains, and not only to have stressed matters which Stuart thought routinary [*sic*] but also to have omitted all reference to other matters which evidently he deemed important."[4] But regardless of merit the translation does prove that Stuart had written the "Travelling Memoranda" by April, 1821.

Equally certain is the earliest possible date of composition. Since he did not complete his journey from St. Louis to New York until late in June, 1813, it was not possible for him to have begun the rewriting of his day-to-day account until this time. The "Travelling Memoranda" is a revised and somewhat enlarged account of the material in another notebook, the "Journal," which Stuart kept while actually traveling. Therefore it could not have been written until he had arrived at his destination and completed the "Journal."

No one knows why Stuart rewrote his diary. In the sales catalogue is the conjecture that it "appears to be the completed copy of the journal written and extended from the rough notes of Robert Stuart jotted down from day to day during this long and terrible journey, for the use and information of John Jacob Astor; and by Mr. Astor turned over to Washington Irving." Rollins adds, "nor do we know why he prepared this narrative—whether as merely a report to Astor or as material deliberately intended for publishment [*sic*]."[5] Stanley T. Williams limits himself to the statement

---

[3] About 26,000 words, compared to 34,000.
[4] *The Discovery of the Oregon Trail,* cviii.
[5] *Ibid.* cviii.

that "this journal was apparently made from the rough notes of Robert Stuart."[6]

Whatever the reason may have been, the "Travelling Memoranda" found its way first to the editors of the *Nouvelles Annales* and then to Pierre and Washington Irving, to be incorporated in the literature of two nations. The French inscription on the page preceding the manuscript proper probably was added in Paris, since the Irvings would have had no reason to use another language. As for Washington Irving, Professor Williams noted that "French or Italian he was never to master, and his stumbling about in the former was to embarrass him until he was well past sixty."[7] Even if Pierre's facility were greater, it seems unlikely that he would prepare a manuscript for his uncle by adding descriptive passages in a tongue with which that uncle was not at ease.

There is, moreover, a factual reason for believing that the phrase was added in Paris rather than in New York. The handwriting is distinctly different from that of either of the Irvings, as well as from that of Robert Stuart. This difference is characteristic of the various jottings that accrued to the manuscript during its passage through unknown hands. A study of letters written by the Irvings at or about the period during which they were working with the "Travelling Memoranda" shows that none of the additions were made by them, the difference in hands being not merely noticeable but marked. Yet the unknown writers all formed their letters after nineteenth rather than twentieth century patterns, an indication that they may have been interested contemporaries.

The substance of these marginal jottings is impersonal. One group consists of annotations of the directions and distances recorded in the textual passages opposite, indicating that the primary interest of the writer lay in tracing the route

[6] *The Life of Washington Irving*, II, 392.
[7] *Ibid.*, I, 45.

that Stuart had followed. Of the 143 notes in this category, all but two are concerned with geographical locations. On page 137 (page 114 above) of the manuscript, opposite the account of McClellan's state at the time he was found by Stuart's party, is the comment, "he left them in the 1st October," while inserted in the text on page 186 (page 148 above) are the words "(Not so)," indicating that Stuart's reference to Grand Island is in error. The second group of marginalia consists of nine pencilings of the abbreviation "Ex^d" on the bottoms of as many pages; apparently it meant "examined." The third is composed of six check marks on as many pages.

Stuart himself employed three types of marks as indicators. The first was a single underline, which he used whenever he departed from what he felt to be standard diction. When referring to buffalo as "black Cattle" he underscored the phrase to show his departure from accepted terminology, in precisely the way that a present-day writer uses quotation marks to set off slang. Local names sometimes were given the same recognition, perhaps from a desire to call attention to the fact that they were not official designations: on page 151 (page 122 above) of the "Travelling Memoranda" is a reference to a mountain "which we call the *big horn*."

A more fruitful type of annotation is the table of distances which runs down the left-hand margin of every page. At the top of the column is the figure giving the accumulated distance from Astoria to that point and at the bottom is the sum derived by adding the day's total to that figure. Scattered between are numbers indicating the miles for each day's travel; if the text contains a statement that the party progressed thirty-two miles, the margin opposite bears the indication "/32/." Checked against modern maps Stuart's figures show what appears at first to be an exaggeration of about 25 per cent. Though the difference may in part be the walker's natural tendency to magnify his distances, unavoidable deviations frequently caused the party to leave the routes now followed by motorists. In 1812 the road to Oregon actually was longer than it is today.

Less useful than Stuart's table of distances is the system of diacritical marks that he employed for a few pages in an attempt to reveal the pronunciation of Indian names. On six occasions he drew in small figure 2's over vowel letters in what appears to have been an attempt to show that they were to be given a short rather than a long sound. If this was his intent, he was following the same system as that which Noah Webster used in his famous blue-backed speller (the *Elementary Spelling Book*) of 1829, where superscribed 2's indicated short vowel sounds. Regardless of his purpose, he used the device only on manuscript pages 28, 29, 32, 34, and 42, leaving his readers to make their own speculations from this point on.

Stuart's notebook is remarkably well preserved. Though it must have passed during the one hundred-odd years of its existence through a number of hands, no pages are missing and very few are loose. The ink, though brown with age, is legible, and the round, well-formed hand in which the words were set down leaves their meaning clear for the present-day reader. Though Stuart's spelling and punctuation are anything but orthodox, his letters are usually so clearly formed that there is no doubt as to what he wants to say. There are occasional obscurities, points at which letters were blurred or omitted, but for the most part the "Travelling Memoranda" remains today what it was at the time that Stuart wrote it: the carefully and honestly inscribed account of a man whose intelligence and character enabled him to transcend his lack of formal training.

Appendix II

Letter by Elisha Loomis

Relating an Account by
Robert Stuart of His Journey

Mackinac *April* 2d 1831

At the meeting of the Mackinac Lyceum last evening Robert Stuart, Esq. gave a brief but interesting account of a voyage to the Pacific Ocean, and journey from the mouth of Columbia River over the Rocky Mountains to New-York. Some of the more prominent facts are worthy of preservation.

In the year 1810 John Jacob Astor of New-York resolved to make a trading establishment at the mouth of Columbia River. For this purpose a vessel was procured and 20 or 30 persons, among whom was Mr. Stewart and an uncle of his, embarked for the above mentioned place. The commander of the ship whose name was Thorn had been a lieutenant in the Navy. He was very self-concieted [*sic*] and extremely irritable. On the very first night he had a quarrel with the passengers—he insisting that they should have no lights after eight o'clock P.M. and that they should go to bed precisely at that hour—while they insisted that they would sit up longer. In consequence of this disagreement there was no cordiality of feeling during the voyage. In crossing the Equator Neptune came on board to shave all the raw hands except such as bribed him to let them off. The shippe stopped some

time at the Falkland Islands, where a plenty of game was
found. When they were about ready to sail Capt. Thorn gave
notice that he should leave at such an hour precisely, and
would fire a gun as a signal—that all must be on board by
the time specified. Most of the passengers, wishing to have
a supply of fresh meat, went out in the morning to hunt. Mr.
S. returned to the vessel about 11 o'clock A.M. His uncle and
5 or 6 others however had not returned at 1 P.M. at which
time the captain fired his gun and set sail notwithstanding it
yet lacked an hour and a half of the time he had set for sailing.
After they had proceeded about 3 miles Mr S. began to grow
uneasy and asked the Capt if he was not going to put back
and take on board the absent men, who were at this time seen
approaching through a heavy sea, in a small canoe they had
found on the shore. The captain swore he would not stop for
them. They might live there he said on the game they could
get, until some vessel touched at the place and took them off.
Mr S., who was at this time quite young, and imprudent, as
well as destitute of religious principle, felt indignant at the
conduct of Capt. T. He went immediately to the cabin, loaded
his pistols, came on deck again and threatened to blow the
Captains brains out unless he would put about the vessel.
After a good deal of alteration [*sic*] the Capt. consented and
took the men on board. At the Sandwch [*sic*] Islands where
they spent some time, the [*sic*] took 20 or 30 of the islanders
to assist them in their contemplated establishment at Columbia River. An instance of the intrepidity of these natives is
worth noticing. A whale following the vessel as is often the
case, and coming close along side, Mr S. handed one of the
natives a knife saying to him in sport at the same time, "Jump
overboard and stab that whale." The native took the knife,
leaped upon the rave [*rail?*] of the vessel and was upon the
point of jumping upon the whale, when he was stopped by
one of the men on board. He said he could plunge the knife

into the whale, and dive immediately so as to escape the blow of the whale. (He would probably have succeeded in this, but the whale in throwing his body over might have struck and seriously injured the vessel. I knew one man who, it was said, once leaped upon the back of a whale, plunging his harpoon into the animal at the same time, and then jumped into the boat, and escaped. In general the whale when struck turns a complete somerset, and dashing to pieces any thing that happens to be where his body falls. On my voyage to the Sandwich Islands, one of our company incautiously discharged a gun loaded with ball into the back of a whale, just as the animal was passing under the bowsprit. In this instance however the whale immediately sunk and disappeared. Had she as is usual thrown her body into the [*vessel?*] the consequence would probably have been the loss of the bowsprit, and perhaps the life of the person who fired the gun.)

On the arrival of the ship (the Tonquin) at Columbia River, the wind was blowing fresh from the sea, which rendered it dangerous to enter. This river is exceedingly difficult of entrance, owing to sand bars. When the wind is from the sea, the waves break nearly over the mouth of the river, and it is difficult to find the proper channel. Capt. Thorne proposed entering immediately, but all the passengers objected, advising him to "lie off and on" a day or too [*sic*] till the violence of the wind should abate. He then said he would send a boat to sound the river. He was told it would be certain death for any one to attempt entering in a boat—that a boat could not "live" in such a sea. All the entreaties and advice of the passengers, however, availed nothing. The Captain was obstinately bent upon the measure. The chief mate and a boat's crew were immediately ordered to enter the river. The passengers, finding their remonstrances with the Captain of none effect, now endeavored to dissuade the men from going telling them they would be justified &c. They however did not dare to disobey the captain. When the boat had got about half a mile from the ship she upset and all on board perished, consisting of the mate and five men. Captain Thorn now felt it necessary to wait a little before entering. Accordingly the vessel stood off from the land. The next morning the wind having abated. The Captain, against the advice of the passengers, despatched another boat into the river. It had proceeded about ¼ of a mile, when the men made a signal that they were in the proper channel. The ship was accordingly steered towards the place. As breakers were observed farther inland, the Captain was entreated to stop and take up the men in the boat, but he refused, saying it would endanger the ship. Some persons however threw a number of ropes to them while the ship was passing. A man caught hold of one of the ropes, but the swiftness of the vessel's motion caused him to let go. They had gone but a little distance when the boat was engulfed in the waves. Two or three days after the vessel had anchored, the indians brought in the bodies of one American and three Sandwich Islanders, still alive although almost dead with cold and fatigue. They were the only survivors of the seven that went in the last boat, and were found by the indians rolled up on the beach, several miles from the river. They said that they succeeded in righting the boat after it was upset and bailing out the water, when the American who was saved and the three Sandwich Islanders got into her. By this time the boat had drifted some distance out to sea, and they accordingly proceeded along the coast some distance, when they were washed on shore at the place where they were found by the Indians. (Remark. Was not Capt. Thorne guilty of the murder of all those men that were lost when the boats upset? Obstinacy, and passion and self-conceit, often lead men into horrible crimes.)

The men who had come for the purpose of forming the establishment commenced building a store and enclosing a small space around with strong pickets to defend themselves from the Indians—Before the pickets were finished Capt Thorne was ready to sail. He was to proceed some hundreds of miles along the coast for the purpose of trade and then return to the river to winter. As he was entirely unacquainted with the manner of trading with the indians it was thought best that one of the partners of the concern should go in the ship with him. Mr Stewart was fixed upon as a suitable person. He accordingly made the necessary preparations, took his trunk to the water's edge, and requested Capt. Thorne, who had at the moment landed, to allow the trunk to be carried aboard in his boat. This the Captain refused, telling him he might get his trunk on board the best way he could. Such conduct in the captain led Mr. S. at once to resolve on remaining with the company at the river. He went back, told the other partners he would not go with Capt Thorn, and that if they would take his advice they would put him in irons &c. One of the partners a Mr M'Cay said he would rather go in the ship than to stay at the river. He accordingly went. After proceeding about 200 miles along the coast the captain stopped to trade. At first all things went on well, till in a dispute with the captain about the price of a certain article, the principal chief told the captain he *lied*, an expression which the indian probably thought very harmless. The captain in anger rubbed an otter skin in the face of the chief and then threw it at him, which was one of the greatest insults that could have been given. The chief immediately got into his canoe with his men and paddled to the shore meditating revenge. As there was no prospect of any farther trade at that place Capt Thorne left the same evening for another place, about 20 miles distant. The Indians on shore collected a number of men at the same time and observing the course of the vessel, kept near shore in their canoes and arrived at the place before the ship. A plan was now laid in conjunction with the indians of that place to take possession of the vessel. On the first arrival of Capt. Thorne at Columbia River, he was very much afraid of the indians and kept up a strict watch but finding the natives apparently friendly, he became careless, and allowed great numbers to come on board at a time. At the place where he now was, the natives, to make sure of the vessel, pretended to be uncommonly friendly, and were willing to trade with out much regard to the price. This conduct in them excited the suspicion of M. Cay who told the Captain he was sure something unfavorable was meditated by the indians. Capt. T. laughed at his fears, told him he was afraid of his life &c. Mr. M'Cay said he was not afraid, but it was duty to be careful and that at any rate he would arm himself. Shortly after an indian whom the captain had brought as an interpreter from Columbia river overheard the indians speaking of their intended attack, and went at once to inform the captain. Capt Thorn, suspecting, unjustly, that he had been induced to say so by Mr M'Cay, told him he was a liar &c. The indian said he was no liar, but if the captain would not take his advice, and keep his men under arms to repel or prevent an attack, he begged he might go on shore, as he should certainly be killed if he stayed on board. Capt. Thorne told him to go as soon as he wished, giving him a kick at the same time. He accordingly left the ship. Just at evening, the Indian chief said to the captain that as he had traded a great deal with him he ought to make him a feast (as was customary) of rice and molasses. To this the captain assented, and when the rice was ready allowed the chief to call on board about 50 young warriors, who he said were his favorites. After they had done eating the chief said they were destitute of knives, and had nothing to skin their otters with but sharp stones. Capt. Thorn gave orders to bring up a whole groce [*sic*] of knives and made them a present of two apiece. They now dispersed themselves all over the deck so as to have two or three indians about each white man, and then the chief gave the signal, by yelling. Instantly the indians sprang upon the crew and officers and overpowered them. Capt. Thorn and Mr M'Cay killed a number of the indians, but were at length slain, when the indians had complete possession of the deck. 4 or 5 men were at this time employed in the rigging. These let down a rope over the hatchway and slid down one by one into the hold, the indians stabbing at them, as they passed with their knives. Though wounded they made their way into the cabin, which they fastened, and then cut holes through which they could fire at those on deck. As they had more than a hundred guns ready loaded they quickly cleared the deck of the indians. As soon as the indians fled, the men came on deck and fired the cannon at them, killing many of them in their canoes. It was now proposed by some to take the long boat and steer for Columbia River. One of the men who was badly wounded objected, saying they would probably be driven on shore, or would die from their wounds in an open boat, before they could reach that place, but that he would cut the cable while they should get the vessel under weigh. To this the others would not agree, saying there were not enough men to manage so large a vessel. The boat accordingly was got ready, and all but the one before mentioned started. This one chose to remain with the ship. The boat had proceeded but a few miles when she was driven on shore. The men fell into the hands of the indians, who, after bringing them to their village, kindled a large fire, killed the men, and feasted on their flesh. In the morning the man who was left with the ship appeared on deck, and made signs of peace to the indians, beckoning to them to come on board. Having learned from the men who were driven ashore in the boat the before mentional particulars, through the indian interpreter whom the captain had set on shore; they came off without fear, knowing as they supposed that one man badly wounded could not hurt them.

When the decks were full of indians this man went below and it is supposed took fire and went to the powder magazine, as the vessel immediately blew up. Such was the fate of the ship Tonquin, Captain Thorne; The indian interpreter from whom these facts were derived returned to Columbia River.

It now became necessary to send an express arcross [*sic*] the continent to New-York, to inform Mr. Astor and the other persons connected with the expedition of the loss of the Tonquin. Mr Stewarts uncle was designated as the leader, and was to be accompanied by three others. Mr. Stewart, the younger, objected to his uncles going on account of his feeble health and the great fatigue and danger he would have to encounter, offering himself to go in his stead. This was finally agreed to.

I have omitted to mention in its place that a part only of the company who left St. Louis, to come by land to Columbia river, arrived in safety, after suffering incredible hardships. A considerable number of them perished on the way.

Mr Stewart and his party proceeded up the Columbia river two or three hundred miles in boats. When at length the navigation became obstructed, they left their boats and proceeded by land. After a while they made a raft and again attempted to proceed by water, but the raft came to pieces and some of the party, among whom was Mr Stewart, fell into the river, and narrowly escaped drowning. Much of their ammunition was also spoiled. They at length purchased horses of the indians and now got along very well. In passing the Rocky Mountains they suffered much for want of food, as little or no game could be found. They would occasionally meet with the Ibex or mountain goat, and with the Antelope. The latter is one of the swiftest of all land animals, and very shy; and yet may be decoyed to within a few rods of the hunter. If you elevate a pole with a red cloth on it, the antelope will approach within a few rods of it, provided the hunter lies concealed. To return to the narrative. Between the different ridges of the mountains there are prairies of 20 or 30 miles in breadth. The party suffered dreadfully for want of water in passing these, as well as in some other instances. They were one day met by a party of 7 or 8 Arapahai indians. They are great thieves. The chief proposed to Mr. Stewart to change horses with him, offering him for the elegant one on which Mr. S. rode, a poor miserable beast. Mr S. declined, as mildly as possible, expecting, however, the indians would be displeased, and endeavor to take his horse by force. This proved to be the case. The chief seized the reins, saying he would have the horse. Mr S. gave the signal to his men to present their pieces, and be ready to fire if he should direct. On presenting their pieces the indians with the exception of the chief above mentioned scampered into the bushes and concealed themselves. The chief now said "it was all play.—He did not want the horse." The parties separated. Mr S., from an acquaintance with the habits of the indians, suspected they would follow in his train, and steal the horses at night. To guard against such a misfortune they fettered their horses, tying their fore legs together, and kept them close to their camp, having one of their party constantly on watch as a centinel. On the seventh or eighth night after their encounter with the indians, when they supposed themselves without doubt safe from depredations, their horses were carried off. It was about day light when one of the men who was on watch thought he saw an indian on horseback at a distance. He gave the alarm, and all the party sprang up. At this time the indian came in full view bearin [*sic*] something like a flag elevated on a pole. He gave a *whoop*, at which all the horses snorted and turned towards him. The whoop was answered by 6 or 7 Indians in the opposite direction, when instantly all the horses started off, towards the indian seen on horseback, notwithstanding their fore feet were tied together. Mr Stewart and party pursued on foot but could not over take them. Presently the 6 or 7

indians came in sight and passed close to them laughing heart-
ily at the success of their plan. They were known to be the
same party that they had before met with. One of them took
pains to turn his backsides towards them in an insulting manner, when an old Kentucky hunter who made one of Mr S s
party drew up his gun to shoot the villain. Mr S. ordered him
to desist. He begged hard to be allowed to shoot once at the
Indian, and even went so far as to offer Mr S. a considerable
part of the wages due him if he would permit him to have
"one crack at the Indian." Mr S. however well knew that such
a measure would arouse the feelings of the whole tribe of
Arapahais, who would then come and kill them all. Destitute
of horses the party hardly knew what to do. Some even proposed to give up all [*hope?*] and die where they were, as it
seemed hardly possible to cross the immense prairies on foot,
weak as they had become and destitute of provesion, knowing
they should find no game on the plains. Indeed they did almost perish. When they had been destitute of food for three
days they discovered an old Buffalo, who had probably retired from the drove to die. He was killed and the men running to him cut off slices of his flesh and *ate it raw.* Afterwards
they cooked and ate as much as they wanted, and much more
than they ought, for they suffered dreadful pain in consequence.

Shortly after this the [*sic*] came to the deserted camp
of a company of Blackfeet indians, who had but just gone,
as their fires were still burning. The Blackfeet tribe made it
their constant practice to put to death every white man except
those connected with the Hudson Bay Company. What a
Providence was here! If their horses had not been stolen
they must have arrived at the camp while the indians were
there and been of course murdered!

After this the [*sic*] found in a *weekwam* an old woman,
who but for their arrival would doubtless have perished, as

she was nearly destitute of provisions, and the men of her tribe were not expected from their hunting excursion for two months. Having recently killed some game, they gave her enough to last until the hunters would return.

Arriving at a tract of woody land and finding Buffalo they concluded to winter there, as the snow had already fallen in considerable quantities. During the winter they were again in great danger from a party of indians then on their way to another tribe, for the purpose of *stealing horses*. This party finally left them after taking all the stock of meat they had laid up for their winter's support.

In the spring the [*sic*] resumed their journey, and on arriving at a trading establishment near the head waters of the Missouri learned that the United States and Great Britian [*sic*] were at *war*, and that all the indians in that vicinity had been withdrawn to assist the British in an attempt to capture Mackinac. This last circumstance was favorable to the party as they would otherwise have been made prisoners. On arriving near the borders of Indiana after having just crossed a river, a white man but a little distance before them was shot dead by an indian on the opposite shore. By this timely warning to Mr Stewart and Co. they were enabled to conceal themselves, and pass out of the reach of the guns.

The preceding contains the principal facts, though not all that were related by Mr Stewart. I have written it under the supposition that it would not be uninteresting, though I freely acknowledge my description is far inferior to the relation given by Mr Stewart. I should not have attempted to repeat what he stated, had any idea that it would have occupied so much paper. I have written it so fast that it has occupied but little of my time.

Yours   E Loomis

Chester Loomis Esq.
Post-Master
Rushville N.Y.

A Selected Bibliography

Books

Brackenridge, Henry Marie. *Views of Louisiana*. Pittsburgh, 1814.

Bradbury, John. *Travels in the Interior of America*. Liverpool, 1817.

Catlin, George. *Catlin's North American Indian Portfolio*. London, 1844 (?); New York, 1845.

———. *Letters and Notes on the Manners, Customs, and Condition of the North American Indians*. 2 vols. London, 1845–48.

Cox, Ross. *Adventures on the Columbia River*. 2 vols. London, 1831.

Ellswoth, Henry L. *Washington Irving on the Prairie, or a Narrative of a Tour of the Southwest in the Year 1832*. Edited by Stanley T. Williams and Barbara D. Simison. New York, 1937.

Franchère, G., *fils*. *Relation d'un Voyage à la Côte du Nord-Quest de L'Amérique Septentrionale, dans les années 1810, 11, 12, 13, et 14*. Montreal, 1820.

———. *Narrative of a Voyage to the Northwest Coast of America in the Years 1811, 1812, 1813, and 1814, or the First American Settlement on the Pacific*. Trans. and ed. by J. V. Huntington. New York, 1854.

Guthrie, A. B., Jr. *The Big Sky.* New York, 1947.

——. *The Way West.* New York, 1949.

Irving, Washington. *A Tour on the Prairies* (included in *The Crayon Miscellany*). Philadelphia, 1835.

——. *Astoria, or Anecdotes of an Enterprise Beyond the Rocky Mountains.* 2 vols. Philadelphia, 1836.

——. *The Rocky Mountains: or, Scenes, Incidents, and Adventures . . . of Capt. B. L. E. Bonneville.* 2 vols. Philadelphia, 1837.

Kane, Paul. *Wanderings of an Artist among the Indians of North America.* London, 1859.

Lewis, Meriwether, and Clark, William. *A History of the Expedition under the Command of Captains Lewis and Clark.* Philadelphia, 1814.

James, Edwin. *Account of an Expedition . . . under the Command of Major Stephen H. Long.* 2 vols. Philadelphia, 1823.

Möllhausen, Baldwin. *Diary of a Journey from the Mississippi to the Coasts of the Pacific.* Trans. by Mrs. Percy Sinnett. London, 1858.

Nouvelles Annales des Voyages, de la Geographie et de l'Histoire ou Recueil des Relations Originals Inédites, Communiquées par des Voyageurs Français et Étrangers. Vol. X contains the Robert Stuart material. Paris, 1821.

Parkman, Francis. *The Oregon Trail.* Boston, 1872.

Pattie, James O. *The Personal Narrative of James O. Pattie, of Kentucky, during an Expedition from St. Louis . . . [to] the Pacific Ocean.* Ed. by Timothy Flint. Cincinnati, 1831.

Rollins, Philip A. *The Discovery of the Oregon Trail.* New York and London, 1935.

Ross, Alexander. *Adventures of the Fist Settlers on the Oregon or Columbia River.* London, 1849.

——. *The Fur Hunters of the Far West.* 2 vols. London, 1855.

Schmölder, Captain B. *Neuer Praktischer Wegweiser für Auswanderer nach Nord-Amerika.* Mainz, 1848.

Thornton, J. Quinn. *Oregon and California in 1848.* 2 vols. New York, 1849.

Travels of Captains Lewis and Clarke, by Order of the Government of the United States. Philadelphia, 1809.

Articles

Anon. "American Enterprise," *Missouri Gazette*, May 15, 1813.

Anon. Description of the "Travelling Memoranda, *American Art Association–Anderson Galleries Catalogue*, Sale No. 2850 (1930), 31–32.

Anon. "Irving's *Astoria*," *The Nation*, Vol. LXV (1897), 499–501.

Burton, R. "Irving's Services to American History," *New England Magazine*, n.s., Vol. XVI (1897).

Crooks, Ramsey. "Col. Frémont and the 'South' Pass," *Detroit Free Press*, July 1, 1856.

Eberstadt, Edward. "The William Robertson Coe Collection of Western Americana," *Yale University Library Gazette*, Vol. III, No. 2 (October, 1948).

Everett, Edward. "Astoria," *North American Review*, Vol. XV (1822), 209–24.

Howard, Joseph K. "Tradition and the Skeptic: Saintly Narcissa and the Blond Barmaid," *Pacific Spectator*, Vol. II (1948), 331–37.

Poe, Edgar Allan. "Astoria," *Southern Literary Messenger*, Vol. III (1837), 59–68.

Russell, John A. "Irving: Recorder of Indian Life," *Journal of American History*, Vol. XXV (1932), 185–95.

Spaulding, Kenneth A. "A Note on Astoria: Irving's Use of the Robert Stuart Manuscript," *American Literature*, Vol. XXII (1950), 150–57.

Street, F. B. "Knickerbocker and the Prairie," Fort Hays, Kansas, State College *Aerend*, Vol. III (1932), 229–30.

Thoburn, Joseph B. "Centennial of the Tour on the Prairies by Washington Irving (1831–1832)," *Chronicles of Oklahoma*, Vol. X (1932), 426–37.

Index

Absaroka: *see* Crow Indians
Alder: 44, 48, 136, 152, 163
Alder Creek (Ore.): 73, 74
American Falls (Ida.): 92, 94
Ammunition: 50, 79, 81, 97, 104, 105, 133
Animals: 49, 81, 82, 138, 139, 143, 163
Antelope: 31, 73, 91, 99, 100, 106, 111, 112, 113, 114, 116, 118, 136, 137
Arapahay Indians: *see* Arapaho Indians
Arapaho Indians: 81, 82, 119, 132, 133, 134
Arms: 40, 46, 50, 64, 78, 79, 81, 89, 97, 101, 104, 111 132
Arrowwood: 153
Ash: 31 44, 48, 136, 137, 152, 158, 163
Ash Creek (Neb.): 145
Aspen: 131
Astoria (Ore.): 27, 64, 88, 164
Astoria, Fort: 28, 46, 63
Auger Falls (Ida.): 88
Auxvasse Creek (Mo.): 163

Badgers: 104
Barges: 27
Baskets: 31
Baths: 39

Beans: 157
Bears: 31, 46, 48, 49, 55, 64, 96, 99, 156, 163
Bear River (Mo.): 81, 95, 97, 99, 102, 131
Bear Creek: *see* Louris Creek
Beavers: 28, 31, 32, 45, 46, 48, 49, 64, 65, 69, 71, 72, 73, 74, 75, 76, 77, 78, 81, 84, 90, 91, 92, 95, 96, 100, 101, 103, 104, 106, 108, 110, 111, 112, 113, 119, 125, 148, 153, 154, 156, 160, 163, 164
Beaver Creek (Neb.): 156
Berger Creek (Mo.): 163
Big Bonne Femme Creek: *see* Bonne Femme Creek
Big Flat: *see* Grande Ronde Valley
Big Horn: *see* antelope
Big Horn River (Wyo.): 81, 120, 132, 133
Big Manitoe Creek: *see* Moniteau Creek
Big Wood River (Ida.): 84
Birch: 48
Black Arm Indians: *see* Ute Indians
Black Snake Hills (Mo.): 206
Blackberries: 31
Blackfeet Indians: 94, 105, 107, 108, 119
Blood: 61
Blueberries: 31

185

Blue Mountains (Ore.): 73
Boats: 27, 46, 47, 52, 160
Boise River (Ida.): 77
Bonne Femme Creek (Mo.): 163
Books: 87, 89
Brady Island (Neb.): 148, 149, 150
Brant: 31, 145
Brownson, Lieutenant John: 162
Bruneau River (Ida.): 82
Buffalo: 79, 95, 113, 116, 118, 119,
  120, 122, 124, 125, 126, 127, 128,
  130, 134, 135, 136, 137, 138, 139,
  140, 141, 143, 144, 145, 147, 148,
  149, 151, 154, 156, 157
Burial, Indian: 34, 117

Cabin de Paille River: *see* Little Blue
  River
Cache: 86, 87, 89, 119, 157
Caldron Linn (Ida.): 87, 88
Callemax: *see* Tillamook Indians
Cannibalism: 114, 115
Canoe: 41, 51, 52, 53, 55, 57, 59, 60,
  61, 62, 86, 87, 88, 90, 129, 134,
  139, 140, 141, 143, 146, 158, 159,
  160, 161
Carson, Alexander: 119
Cascade Creek: *see* Big Wood River
Casper Range (Wyo.): 131, 135
Cass, Martin: 83
Cathlasko (Echeloot) Indians: 58, 61
Cath-lath-la-la (Echeloot) Indians:
  53
Cath-lack-la Indians: 48
Cath-lak-a-heckit (Echeloot) Indians:
  53
Cathlakamaps (Cathlamet) Indians:
  47
Cathlamet Indians (extinct): 42
Cathlapootle (Cathlapotle) Indians:
  47
Cath-la-poo-quaa Indians (extinct):
  48
Cave-in Rock: *see* Tavern Rock
Cedar: 30, 41, 52, 91, 106, 117, 126,
  127, 131, 137, 138, 144, 145
Cedar Creek: *see* Ash Creek
Cedar River: *see* Willow River

Celillo Falls (Ore.): 52, 55, 58, 59,
  65, 66, 88
Champlain, Jean Baptiste: 119
Charette Creek (Mo.): 163
Chariton River (Mo.): 162
Chee-hee-lish (Chehalis) Indians: 28,
  45
Cheepan-chick-chick (Echeloot) In-
  dians: 58
Cherries, wild: 31, 94
Cheyenne Indians: 128
Cheyenne River (Wyo.): 102, 120,
  128, 129
Chief's Knife: 156
Chieftainship: 36
Chiefs: 36
Chi-hee-leesh: *see* Chee-hee-lish
Chilwit (Echeloot) Indians: 44, 58
Chinook, Point (Ore.): 28
Chinook Indians: 28, 29
Chokecherries: 31
Chub: 32, 65, 89
Clappin's Rapid (Ida.): 88
Clarke, John: 27, 55, 57, 66, 67
Clatsop, Fort (Ore.): 27
Clatsop Indians: *see* interpreter
Clay: 30, 119
Clearwater River (Ida.): 72
Clemson, Major Eli: 161, 208
Clerks: 27
Columbia River: 28, 48, 52, 58, 63,
  66, 67, 76, 81, 120, 146, 152, 153
Conger: *see* eels
Copperas: 123
Cordilleras: *see* Rocky Mountains
Corn: 148, 157
Cornfield Creek: *see* Horse Creek
Cottonwood: 31, 44, 48, 69, 72, 93,
  97, 100, 106, 111, 117, 128, 134,
  135, 136, 137, 144, 150, 152, 158,
  163
Council: 55, 62
Courtship: 34, 35
Cow-lit-sic (Cowlitz) River (Ore.):
  46
Cowlitz Indians: *see* Le-cow-lit-sic
Cranberries: 31
Creation myth: 33

Creepers: 31
Crime: 36
Crooks, Ramsey: 27, 64, 75, 77, 87, 88, 107, 109, 110, 111, 118, 157
Cross Creek: *see* Granite Creek
Crow Creek: 98
Crow Indians: 78, 97, 98, 99, 101, 102, 103, 107, 116, 118, 119, 120, 121, 122, 132, 133, 134
Crows: 32
Curlews: 32, 153
Currants: 31

Dancing: 39, 62, 66
Day, John: 27, 45, 46, 47, 64
Death: 62, 63
Deer: 28, 31, 40, 46, 48, 49, 55, 64, 65, 72, 104, 127, 128, 130, 131, 132, 137, 148, 149, 153, 154, 155, 156, 161, 163
Deer Island (Ore.): 46
Delauney, Pierre: 119
Derangement: 45, 46, 47
Deschutes River (Ore.): 62
Detayé, Pierre: 119
Devil's Gate (Wyo.): 126
Devil's Scuttle Hole: *see* Caldron Linn
Dews: 29
Disappointment, Cape (Wash.): 27
Dogs: 31, 40, 67, 91
Dogwood: 163
Domestic animals: 31
Doruin, François: 157, 158
Dress, Indian: 30, 41, 48, 62
Ducks: 31, 45, 112, 145
Dung: 124, 144, 148

Eagles: 32
East Fork River (Wyo.): 118
Eber's Creek: *see* Sniabar Creek
Echeloot Indians: *see* Cathlasko, Cathlath-la-la, Cath-lak,aheckit, Cathlakamaps, Cheepan-chick-chick, Chilwit, *and* Ilth-kye-manit Indians
Eels: 32, 65
Ehnenger, George: 27
Elk: 28, 29, 31, 40, 46, 49, 72, 105, 110, 128, 149, 154, 156, 163

Elk Horn River (Neb.): 160
Elm: 163
Emigrants: 164

Factories: 162
Falls Creek: *see* Portneuf River
Fiery Prairies Creek: *see* Fire Creek
Fir: 131
Fire Creek (Mo.): 162
Fire deity: *see* gods
Fish: 32, 33, 48, 49, 69, 80, 81, 163
Fish Indians: 63
Fisheries: 54, 58, 66, 74, 77, 103
Five Mile Rapids (Ore.): 55, 59, 63
Flies: 79, 80
Flathead Indians: 76
Flattening of the head: 38
Floats: 48
Flour: 92
Fogs: 29
Forks (of the Columbia): 27, 58
Fort Astoria: *see* Astoria, Fort
Fort Clapsop: *see* Clatsop, Fort
Fort Osage: *see* Osage, Fort
Fowl: 28, 49, 145, 149, 153
Foxes: 31
Frogs: 32

Game Hill (Wyo.): 112
Games: 39, 40
Gasconade River (Mo.): 163
Geese: 31, 45, 96, 142, 145, 146, 152
Gifts: 63, 78, 79, 118, 133
Glaize River: *see* Grande Ronde River
Gods: 33, 34
Gooseberries: 31
Governor, New Archangel: 45
Grand Charaton River: *see* Chariton River
Grand Island (Neb.): 148, 149, 150, 152, 154
Grand Rapids: *see* Upper Cascades
Grande Ronde River (Ore.): 70, 71, 72
Grande Ronde Valley (Ore.): 70, 71, 76
Granite Creek (Wyo.): 112

Grass: 83, 84, 86, 87, 96, 124, 138, 144, 152, 154, 155
Gray, Captain Robert: 42
Great Britain: 158
Green River (Wyo.): 102, 113, 114, 116, 117, 119, 120, 121, 133
Grey's River (Wyo.): 100
Grizzlies: 31, 110, 131
Grouse: 32
Gulls: 32
Gum: 52

Hackberry: 163
Hair: 38
Hamilton Island (Ore.): 49, 51, 53
Hazel, shrub: 48
Hawaiians: 27
Hawthorn: 106
Health: 41, 42
Hecate's Caldron: *see* Caldron Linn
Hemlock: 30
Henry's Fork (Ida.): 89, 108
Henry's Fort (Ida.): 80, 94, 102, 106, 134
Henry's Hill: *see* Game Hill
Herons: 32
Hickory: 158, 163
Hides: *see* skins
Hoback, John: 80, 89, 112
Hoback River (Wyo.): 112
Homicide: 36
Hood, Mt. (Ore.): 63
Horse Creek (eastern Neb.): 156
Horse Creek (western Neb.): 138, 139, 140, 143
Horse Creek (Wyo.): 111
Horses: 31, 62, 65, 66, 67, 68, 76, 78, 79, 81, 82, 83, 84, 86, 93, 95, 96, 97, 99, 100, 101, 102, 118, 120, 124, 125, 126, 127, 132, 134, 138, 142, 143, 151, 152, 153, 154, 158
Horses, wild: 145, 148
Hot Lake (Ore.): 71, 72
Hot springs (Ida.): 107
Houses: 39, 49, 63, 77, 118, 130, 132, 133, 138, 141, 151, 159, 160
Hunt, Wilson: 27, 75, 78, 86, 107

Hunter's Fork: *see* Jack Creek
Hunting, Indian: 40, 41, 66

Ibex: *see* antelope
Idols: 33, 34
Ilth-kye-mamit Indians: 58
Interpreter: 55, 57

Jack Creek (Wyo.): 112
John Day River (Ore.): 64
Jones, Benjamin: 27, 89, 90, 100, 103, 104, 110, 125, 127, 154, 155
Juan de Fuca, Straits of (Wash.): 46
Juniper: 31

Kansas Indians: 162, 164
Kansas River (Kan.): 162
Kentucky: 164

La Chapelle, André: 119
Lamine River (Mo.): 162
Landry, François: 119
Language (coastal Indians): 41
Laramie Peak (Wyo.): 135
Laramie Range (Wyo.): 135
Laramie River (Wyo.): 137
Larks: *see* Oldfield larks
Leather: *see* skins
Leclaire, François: 27, 67, 113, 114, 120, 127, 140
Leclerc, François: *see* Leclaire
Le-cow-lit-six (Cowlitz) Indians: 46
Letters: 90
Lewis River: *see* Snake River
Lewis (Captain Meriwether) and Clark (Captain William): 27, 47
Little Auxvasse Creek (Mo.): 163
Little Blue River (Mo.): 162
Little Bonne Femme Creek (Mo.): 163
Little Manitoe Creek (Mo.): 163
Little Neemahaa River: *see* Little Nemaha River
Little Nemaha River (Mo.): 161
Little River Platte: *see* Platte River
Little Salmon River (Ida.): 75
Little Tarkio River (Mo.): 161
Lizards: 32

Long Hair, Chief: 156
Long Narrows: *see* Five Mile Rapids
Loup Indians: 156
Loup River (Neb.): 148, 154, 156
Louris Creek (Mo.): 163
Loutre Creek (Mo.): 163
Loutre River: *see* Loutre Creek
Lower Cascades (Ore.): 50, 51

McClellan, Robert: 27, 60, 75, 87, 108, 112, 114, 122, 141
McDougall, Duncan: 27
McKay Creek (Ore.): 69
McKay's River (Ore.): 47
McKenzie, Donald: 27, 48, 49, 66, 75
Mad River: *see* Snake River
Mad River Mountain: *see* Teton Pass
Magpies: 32
Map: 134
Marriage (coastal Indians): 34, 35
Marsh Creek (Ida.): 91, 94
Mathlarobe Indians: *see* Watlala Indians
Meat: 103, 104, 105, 106, 108, 114, 130, 133, 151, 153; venison, 33, 66; buffalo, 97, 116, 118, 141; antelope, 112; wolf, 112
Medicine: 33, 34, 109, 110; medicine man (coastal Indians), 34; medicine lodge, 117; medicine bags, 160
Middle Loup River (Neb.): 156
Miller, Joseph: 80, 85, 89, 93, 94, 95, 96, 103, 133, 145
Mississippi River: 163
Missouri Indians: 159, 163
Missouri River: 119, 120, 123, 129, 134, 146, 160, 163, 164
Moccasins: 105, 118, 133
Moniteau Creek (Mo.): 163
Moody Creek (Ida.): 106
Moose deer: *see* elk
Moreau Creek (Mo.): 163
Mosquitoes: 78, 79, 80
Muddy Creek: *see* Salmon Falls Creek
Muddy Creek (Wyo.): 125
Muddy Gap (Wyo.): 125
Mulberry: 163
Mulpat River: *see* Little Salmon River

Multnomah Falls (Ore.): 49
Multnomah River (Ore.): 47
Music: 39
Muskrats: 29, 31

Nets, fish: 54
New Archangel, Alaska: 45
New Fork River (Wyo.): 116
New Mexico: 157
New York: 164
New Year's Day: 141
Nez Percé Indians: 76
Niobrara River (Neb.): 129, 134, 139
Neshnabotna River (Mo.): 161
Nodaway River (Mo.): 161
North Loup River (Neb.): 156
North Platte River: 126, 127, 128, 129, 130, 132, 134, 135, 136, 137, 138, 139, 140, 142, 143, 144, 145, 146, 147, 148, 149, 150, 151, 152, 153, 154, 155, 156, 157, 158, 159, 160, 161, 162, 163, 164

Oak: 31, 44, 46, 48, 63, 136, 158, 161, 163
Oars: 160
Oldfield larks: 153
Old Little Osage Village (Mo.): 162
Osage Indians: 162, 164
Osage, Fort (Mo.): 158, 161, 162
Osage River (Mo.): 162, 163
Otoe Indians: 148, 151, 152, 155, 156, 157, 158, 159, 163
Otters: 28, 31, 32, 40, 65, 160, 163
Otto Indians: *see* Otoe Indians

Padeau Fork: *see* North Loup River
Paints, Indian: 126
Panthers: 31
Partridges: 32
Patriarchs: 36
Papaw: 163
Pawnee Indians: 148, 151, 154, 156, 157, 158, 159, 162
Pelicans: 32
Pens, Indian: 142, 143
Pheasants: 32, 146

Physical characteristics (Indian): 37
Pigeons: 32
Pilot Knobs: *see* Teton Range
Pine: 46, 49, 63, 91, 95, 96, 106, 111,
    117, 118, 131, 137, 144, 151
Pipe of peace: 63, 119
Plains: 65, 91
Planters: 164
Platte River (Mo.): 162
Platte River (Wyo. and Neb.): *see*
    North Platte
Plum Creek (Neb.): 156, 160
Point George: *see* George, Point
Poison Spider Creek (Wyo.): 128,
    130
Poligamy: 35, 36
Pomme de terre: 153
Pomme de Terre River: *see* Middle
    Loup River
Ponca Indians: 129
Portage Falls: *see* American Falls
Portages: 49, 52, 53, 56, 57, 59, 60,
    61, 64, 104
Portneuf River (Ida.): 93, 94, 95
Powder River (Ore.): 73
Prairies: 46, 87, 95, 138, 144, 149,
    153, 155
Prairie dogs: 135
Precipice Creek: *see* Rock Creek
Presents: *see* gifts
Prickly pears: 148
Privations: 164
Property, division of (coastal In-
    dians): 34, 35
Providence: 103, 157
Puget's or Gass' Deer Island: *see* Deer
    Island
Pumpkins: 157

Quick Sand River: *see* Sandy River

Raccoons: 72, 163
Rafts: 90, 103, 104, 105, 111
Raft River (Ida.): 92
Rainier, Mt. (Wash.): 46
Rains: 29, 30, 67
Rapid River: *see* Niobrara River
Raspberries: 31

Rattlesnakes: 32
Ravens: 32
Reed, John: 59, 60, 61, 62, 90
Religion: 33
Republican Indians: 162, 164
Reptiles: 32
Reznor, Jacob: 80, 89, 90
Rice: 89
Ringing Water River: *see* Plum Creek
Robes: *see* skins, buffalo
Robinson, Edward: 80, 89, 90
Roche Percé Creek (Mo.): 163
Rocky Creek (Ida.): 86
Rocky Bluff Creek: *see* Bruneau River
Rocky Mountains: 30, 52, 76, 81, 95
Roi, Baptiste: 158
Roots: 32, 66, 78, 79, 91, 96, 153
Rosinante: 142, 143
Russian establishments: 45

Sacrifices: 33, 34
Sage: 91, 92
St. John's Creek (Mo.): 163
St. Louis: 64, 158, 162, 164
St. Michel, Louis: 119
Saline River: *see* Salt Creek
Salmon: 29, 32, 33, 42, 43, 48, 54,
    58, 70, 71, 77, 79, 81, 82, 84, 85,
    91, 93
Salmon Falls (Ida.): 84
Salmon Falls Creek (Ida.): 85
Salmon River (Ida.): 72
Salt: 121
Salt Creek (Neb.): 158, 160
Salt River (Wyo.): 99, 100
Salt wood: 77, 91
Sand: 91, 144, 145, 146
Sandwich Islanders: *see* Hawaiians
Sandy River (Ore.): 49
Sawyers: 164
Scyatoga Indians: *see* Nez Percé
Seals: 40, 49
Seal Rocks (Ore.): 49
Serviceberries: 32, 91, 94
Settlements: 164
Shells: 122
Shepherd's Creek (Mo.): *see* Berger
    Creek

Index

Shooshonie River (Ore.): *see*
  Deschutes River
Shoo-shoo-nay Indians: *see* Shoshone
  Indians
Shoshone Indians: 48, 57, 63, 77, 80,
  81, 82, 83, 84, 91, 93, 98, 102,
  118, 121
Signals: 97
Sinews: 160
Sioux Indians: 129
Skins: 49, 133, 134, 145, 147, 158,
  159, 160, 163; bear, 29; elk, 29, 48,
  160; muskrat, 41; deer, 41, 48,
  130; beaver, 43, 48, 75, 157; ante-
  lope, 75, 130; buffalo, 97, 129, 130,
  134, 145, 157, 160
Skull, buffalo: 117
Sloes: 31
Smallpox: 47
Smelt: 32
Snake Indians: *see* Shoshone Indians
Snake River (Ida.): 66, 72, 74, 75,
  76, 77, 79, 80, 82, 83, 85, 86, 87,
  88, 89, 92, 93, 94, 99, 100, 102,
  103, 104, 105, 106, 109, 111, 119
Snakes: 32
Sniabar Creek (Mo.): 162
Snipe: 32
Snow: 30, 76, 105, 108, 109, 118,
  120, 122, 124, 126, 130, 134, 135,
  137, 138, 139, 143, 154, 158
Snowshoes: 158
Soil: 30, 64, 67, 91, 93, 94, 106,
  146, 154, 163
Songs: 62
Song birds: 32
Soule, Captain: *see* Sowles, Cornelius
South Platte River: 132, 147, 148
Sowles, Cornelius: 27
Spanish River: *see* Green River
Spanish territory: 82
Spears: 33
Split Rock Creek: *see* Roche Percé
  Creek
Spring Creek (Ida.): 98
Spruce: 30
Squaws: 151, 154
Stone-toater: 96

Straw: 146, 148, 159
Strawberry Island: *see* Hamilton
  Island
Strawberries: 31
Stuart, David: 27, 51, 59, 60
Stuart, Robert: 27
Sturgeon: 32, 33, 45, 48
Sulphur Lake: *see* Hot Lake
Swamps: 28, 32, 69, 94, 100, 145,
  148, 149, 151
Swans: 31, 45, 145, 146, 152
Sweetwater River (Wyo.): 125, 126
Sycamores: 163

Tabeau's River: *see* Tabo Creek
Tabo Creek (Mo.): 162
Tarkio River (Mo.): 161
Tavern Rock: (Mo.): 163
Temperature: 30
Ten Mile Rapids (Ore.): 57
Teton Pass (Ida. and Wyo.): 78, 111
Teton Range (Wyo.): 109, 110, 111
Teton River (Ida.): 108, 111
Theft: 36, 40, 59, 64, 76, 79, 97,
  101, 102
Thomas Fork of Bear River (Ida.):
  97
Tillamook Indians: 28
Toads: 32
Tobacco: 57, 63, 119, 141
Toe: *see pomme de terre*
Tongue Point (Ore.): 27
Trail Creek (Ida.): 111
Traps: 89, 103, 104, 108, 113
Treachery: 36
Trout: 32, 89, 92, 96, 103, 112
Trout Run: *see* Raft River
Turcotte, Jean: 119
Turkey: 157, 161, 163
Turtles: 32
Twine: 52

Umatilla River (Ore.): 65, 67, 69
United States: 161
Upper Cascades (Ore.): 49, 52, 53,
  59, 63
Urine: 67
Ute Indians: 82

Uthlathglagla: 33
Uthlechan: 33, 45

Vache, la: *see* buffalo
Vallée, André: 27, 104, 112, 120, 153, 157
Vancouver's Point (Wash.): 49
Venison: *see* meat, venison
Villages: *see* Old Little Osage Village
Vines: 31
Volcanic formations: 122
Vultures: 32

Waak-i-cum Indians: *see* Wahkiacum Indians
Wahkiacum Indians: 42
Wallamat: *see* Willamette River
Walla Walla Indians: 65, 66
Walla Walla River (Ore.): 65, 66, 67, 87, 90
Wallowa Mountains (Ore.): 72
Walnut: 31, 46, 48, 163
Wapatoes: 45, 152
War: 37, 61, 157, 158, 161, 164
War bags: 160
Watlala Indians: 47
Weapons: 36, 40, 59

Weather: 29–31
Weiser's River (Ida.): 78
Whortleberries: 31
Wildcats: 163
Willamette Falls (Ore.): 48
Willamette River (Ore.): 47, 48, 49, 76
Willow: 31, 72, 73, 74, 77, 80, 84, 85, 86, 91, 92, 100, 106, 108, 117, 118, 120, 125, 126, 128, 134, 136, 147, 148, 149, 150, 151, 152, 153, 159, 160
Willow River (Neb.): 156
Wind River Mountains (Wyo.): 118, 120
Winds: 30
Winslip, Captain Nathan: 44
Wolf Creek (Mo.): 161
Wolverines: 104
Wolves: 31, 87, 112
Woodpeckers: 32
Wood-pile-creek: *see* Burnt River
Woods Creek: *see* St. John's Creek
Wormwood: 91
Wounds: 61, 62

Yellowstone River (Mont.): 132

The type used in this book is Caslon Old Face, a Linotype version of a type design created about 1720 by William Caslon of London. The American colonies, until the revolution, depended almost entirely on type from Caslon's foundry and a few others in England, though domestic manufacture was becoming established by the time Robert Stuart made the trip recorded here, the first known American type specimen book appearing in 1812.

The signs of the zodiac which introduce the various months were chosen as decorations because a knowledge of the position of the stars and planets was of great importance to early nineteenth-century travelers across the unmarked continent.

University of Oklahoma Press
Norman